Congressional Research Service

War in Afghanistan: Strategy, Military Operations, and Issues for Congress

Steve Bowman
Specialist in National Security

Catherine Dale
Specialist in International Security

May 6, 2010

Congressional Research Service

7-5700

www.crs.gov

R40156

CRS Report for Congress ———————————————
Prepared for Members and Committees of Congress

c11173008

Report Documentation Page

1. REPORT DATE **06 MAY 2010**	2. REPORT TYPE	3. DATES COVERED **00-00-2010 to 00-00-2010**

4. TITLE AND SUBTITLE **War in Afghanistan: Strategy, Military Operations, and Issues for Congress**	5a. CONTRACT NUMBER
	5b. GRANT NUMBER
	5c. PROGRAM ELEMENT NUMBER
6. AUTHOR(S)	5d. PROJECT NUMBER
	5e. TASK NUMBER
	5f. WORK UNIT NUMBER

7. PERFORMING ORGANIZATION NAME(S) AND ADDRESS(ES) **Congressioinal Research Service,Library of Congress,101 Independence Ave., SE,Washington,DC,20540-7500**	8. PERFORMING ORGANIZATION REPORT NUMBER

9. SPONSORING/MONITORING AGENCY NAME(S) AND ADDRESS(ES)	10. SPONSOR/MONITOR'S ACRONYM(S)
	11. SPONSOR/MONITOR'S REPORT NUMBER(S)

12. DISTRIBUTION/AVAILABILITY STATEMENT
Approved for public release; distribution unlimited

13. SUPPLEMENTARY NOTES

14. ABSTRACT

15. SUBJECT TERMS

16. SECURITY CLASSIFICATION OF:			17. LIMITATION OF ABSTRACT	18. NUMBER OF PAGES	19a. NAME OF RESPONSIBLE PERSON
a. REPORT **unclassified**	b. ABSTRACT **unclassified**	c. THIS PAGE **unclassified**	**Same as Report (SAR)**	**76**	

Summary

With a deteriorating security situation and no comprehensive political outcome yet in sight, most observers view the war in Afghanistan as open-ended. By early 2009, a growing number of Members of Congress, Administration officials, and outside experts had concluded that the effort—often called "America's other war"—required greater national attention. For the Government of the Islamic Republic of Afghanistan (GIRoA), the war is both a struggle for survival and an effort to establish sustainable security and stability. For the United States, the war in Afghanistan concerns the security of Afghanistan and the region, including denying safe haven to terrorists and helping ensure a stable regional security balance. For regional states, including India and Russia as well as Afghanistan's neighbors Pakistan and Iran, the war may have a powerful impact on the future balance of power and influence in the region. For individual members of the North Atlantic Treaty Organization (NATO), the war may be about defeating terrorist networks, ensuring regional stability, proving themselves as contributing NATO members, and/or demonstrating NATO's relevance in the 21st century.

Since 2001, the character of the war in Afghanistan has evolved from a violent struggle against al Qaeda and its Taliban supporters to a multi-faceted counterinsurgency (COIN) effort. In the aftermath of the terrorist attacks of September 11, 2001, the United States launched Operation Enduring Freedom (OEF) in order to end the ability of the Taliban regime to provide safe haven to al Qaeda and to put a stop to al Qaeda's use of the territory of Afghanistan as a base of operations for terrorist activities. In that first phase, U.S. and coalition forces, working with Afghan opposition forces, quickly removed the Taliban regime.

After the fall of the Taliban, the character of the war shifted to a multifaceted COIN effort aimed at smothering the diffuse insurgency by shoring up GIRoA efforts to provide security, governance, and economic development. The three areas are generally viewed as interdependent and mutually-reinforcing—security is a prerequisite for some governance and development efforts, and longer-term, sustainable security requires both functional governance and economic opportunity. As one pillar of the COIN campaign in Afghanistan, the Afghan and international military effort aims broadly at defeating the remnants of the Taliban and other insurgents, securing the population, and helping extend the reach of the Afghan government. The international military effort includes both the NATO-led International Security Assistance Force (ISAF), to which the United States contributes troops, and the separate U.S.-led OEF mission.

In his December 3, 2009, speech President Obama identified several objectives in Afghanistan and Pakistan: (1) disrupt, dismantle, and defeat al Qaeda; (2) deny al Qaeda a safe haven; (3) reverse the Taliban's momentum and deny it the ability to overthrow the government; and (4) strengthen the capacity of the Afghan security forces and government to better protect and serve population centers. To accomplish this, President Obama ordered the deployment of an additional 30,000 troops to the region, which will bring the U.S. total to almost 100,000 troops. This deployment will be staged over several months, with the full additional complement being in-country by the end of the summer 2010. Noting that Afghan operations continue to be an international effort, President Obama expressed confidence that some of 42 coalition allies will also be increasing their contributions. NATO Secretary-General Rasmussen echoed this confidence, stating that he expects NATO allies to contribute at least an additional 5,000 troops in 2010.

This report will be updated as events warrant.

Contents

Figures

Contacts

Overview

Unlike the war in Iraq, which, many argue, has entered its endstate, the war in Afghanistan—where the security situation has deteriorated and no comprehensive political outcome is yet in sight—appears to many observers to be open-ended. By early 2009, a growing number of Members of Congress, Administration officials, and outside experts had concluded that the effort—often called America's "other war"—required greater national attention.[1] In his inaugural address, President Obama stated that the United States would "forge a hard-earned peace in Afghanistan."[2]

For the government of Afghanistan, the war is first of all an existential struggle for survival against the Taliban and other insurgents, as well as a longer-term effort to establish sustainable security and stability. For the U.S. government, the war in Afghanistan concerns the security of both Afghanistan and the region, including denying safe haven to terrorists and helping ensure a constructive and stable regional security balance.[3] For regional states, including India and Russia as well as Afghanistan's immediate neighbors Pakistan and Iran, the war is critical because it may have a powerful impact on the future security and balance of power and influence in the region. For individual member states of the NATO Alliance, the war may be about some combination of defeating terrorist networks, ensuring regional stability, proving themselves as contributing NATO members, and demonstrating the relevance of the Alliance to 21st century security challenges.

The U.S. government continues to face major strategic and operational decisions about its engagement in the war in Afghanistan. Elements of the debate that continue to attract attention include

- defining U.S. national interests in Afghanistan and the region;

- defining clear strategic objectives and a desired end-state based on those interests;

- determining which diplomatic, economic, and military approaches to adopt, and what resources to commit to support those approaches;

- prioritizing the Afghanistan war versus other national security imperatives including the war in Iraq and preparing to meet potential threats; and

---

[1] See for example the replies to questions for the record, submitted by Secretary of State nominee Hillary Clinton to the Senate Foreign Relations Committee (SFRC), for her January 13, 2009, confirmation hearing, available at http://www.foreignpolicy.com/files/KerryClintonQFRs.pdf; and replies to questions for the record, submitted by Under Secretary of Defense for Policy nominee Michèle Flournoy to the Senate Armed Services Committee (SASC), for her January 15, 2009, confirmation hearing, available at http://armed-services.senate.gov/statemnt/2009/January/ Flournoy%2001-15-09.pdf. See also Joseph J. Collins, "Afghanistan: Faltered But Not Fallen," *Armed Forces Journal*, January 2009; Michael O'Hanlon, "Playing for Keeps," *USA Today*, January 7, 2009; Nathaniel C. Fick and John A. Nagl, "Counterinsurgency Field Manual: Afghanistan Edition," *Foreign Policy*, January/ February 2009.

[2] President Barack Obama, Inaugural Address, January 20, 2009, text available at http://www.whitehouse.gov/blog/ read_the_inaugural_address/.

[3] In her replies to questions for the record, submitted to the Senate Foreign Relations Committee (SFRC) for her January 13, 2009, confirmation hearing, Secretary of State nominee Hillary Clinton stated: "President-Elect Obama and I believe that Afghanistan and the Pakistani border are the central front in the war on terror." See text available at http://www.foreignpolicy.com/files/KerryClintonQFRs.pdf.

- helping marshal a coordinated application of international efforts.

Avenues available to Congress for exercising oversight of these issues include authorizing and appropriating funding for U.S. efforts in Afghanistan and the region; shaping policy through directive legislation; confirming senior administration officials with responsibility for the Afghanistan effort; holding oversight hearings to assess policy formulation and execution; and extending or adjusting Administration reporting requirements.[4]

Recent Developments

Report on Progress Toward Security and Stability in Afghanistan

In April, the Administration submitted the *Report on Progress Toward Security and Stability in Afghanistan*, the fifth in a congressionally mandated semi-annual series. With regard to military operations, selected highlights of the report include the following:

- The deployment of additional U.S. forces is expected to be completed in August 2010, bringing the total to about 98,000. NATO and allied countries have pledged over 9, 000 additional troops, for a coalition total of about 150,000 personnel.

- Many coalition national leaders have noted the lack of public support in their countries for the Afghanistan mission, which has curtailed their ability to meet agreed upon force requirements.

- The ISAF HQ has identified 80 Afghan districts as "key terrain," with anther 41 being designated as "Areas of Interest." These are areas of concentrated population and economic importance, whose stabilization will be the primary focus of ISAF operations.

- To improve the unity of command, Central Command HQ has transferred operational control (OPCON) of almost all U.S. forces to ISAF's General McChriystal, retaining operational control of a small special operations personnel.

- The creation of competent Afghan National Security Forces, both the army and the national police, remains a very high ISAF priority; however, there are significant challenges with regard to recruitment, retention, and corruption, particularly with regard to the police force. Efforts have also been hampered by a notable shortfall in trainers.

- Though levels of violence in the country are significantly higher than this period last year, owing to the increased tempo of military operations, polls indicate that a majority of the Afghan population believe the security situation has improved.

---

[4] For example, the *National Defense Authorization Act for Fiscal Year 2008*, P.L. 110-181, January 28, 2008, §1230 required a "report on progress toward security and stability in Afghanistan," no later than 90 days after enactment and every 180 days thereafter until the end of FY2010. That report is to include a "comprehensive strategy of the United States for security and stability in Afghanistan" that addresses NATO and its International Security Assistance Force (ISAF), the Afghan National Security Forces (ANSF), Provincial Reconstruction Teams (PRTs) and other development initiatives, counter-narcotics activities, the rule of law, and regional considerations. P.L. 110-181, §1231, required, no later than 90 days after enactment, and annually to the end of FY2010, a report on sustaining the Afghanistan National Security Forces.

Operation Moshtarak

On February 13 in Helmand province, ISAF and Afghan forces undertook the largest joint military offensive to date. The 2nd U.S. Marine Expeditionary Brigade composes the bulk of ISAF's 7,000 troops in the offensive, with the Afghan National Army and the Afghan National Civil Order Police providing an additional 8,000 personnel.[5] Intended to regain control of an area long-held by the Taliban, *Operation Moshtarek* is widely viewed as a crucial test of current counterinsurgency strategy. ISAF officials have repeatedly emphasized the importance of Afghan participation in all facets of the operation, from planning through execution. This includes not only Afghan military forces but also administrative elements of the central government brought in behind the military offensive to take over the political and economic rehabilitation of the region. To date, the offensive has encountered only sporadic active resistance, though some encounters with insurgents have been intense, particularly in the area of Marjah. Many insurgents are believed to have fled the area in advance, leaving behind an extensive array of improvised explosive devices. ISAF commanders have indicated that they expect it to take 25-30 days to complete the military objectives, and another six months to judge the overall success in wresting control of the region from the Taliban. Unlike previous occasions, following active combat operations ISAF and Afghan military/police forces will remain to provide security for the population, the governmental administration, and those undertaking the economic reconstruction of the region. If operations go as expected, it is anticipated that within the next six months a similar effort will be undertaken in neighboring Kandahar province.[6]

London Conference/Istanbul Conference

In January, representatives of more than 60 nations met at the International Conference on Afghanistan in London, pledging support and resources to the increased personnel objective and accelerated timeline for the development of Afghan National Security Forces, and announcing new commitment of troops and trainers to ISAF (see "ISAF Troop Contributions" section).

In February NATO Defense Ministers met in Istanbul to discuss alliance funding issues, and Secretary Gates continued his efforts to encourage greater allied participation in Afghan operations. Though NATO nations have already committed to sending an additional 9,000 troops to Afghanistan, the Administration would like to obtain additional commitments for up to 4,000 more mentors and trainers for the Afghan National Security Forces.[7]

Strategy Review and Conclusions

The Obama Administration conducted a wide-ranging review of the strategy options and resource requirements for operations in Afghanistan, and the President presented his decisions in a speech at the U.S. Military Academy on December 1, 2009. Ongoing since August, this review was undertaken in response to an initial assessment of the security situation in Afghanistan submitted by General McChrystal, commander of the U.S./NATO International Security Assistance Force, and in response to concerns raised by charges of widespread corruption in the recent Afghan presidential election. Though classified, General McChrystal's report was leaked to the press and

---

[5] NATO-ISAF Briefing,, Maj. Gen. Nick Carter, February 18, 2010.

[6] Ibid.

[7] "Gates Asks NATO for More Trainers and Mentors," American Forces Press Service, February 4, 2010.

subsequently a redacted unclassified version was released by the Administration.[8] The report assessed the security situation in Afghanistan to be deteriorating, with a growing insurgency whose momentum must be turned within 12 months or risk the possibility it could not be defeated. His principal recommendation was a shift in strategy from an emphasis on offensive military operations to a more comprehensive counterinsurgency strategy, which would seek to protect the population from both insurgent violence and inadvertent harm from allied military operations, while accelerating the training and reliance upon Afghan National Security Forces. At the same time General McChrystal emphasized the importance of stemming the endemic corruption of the Afghan central government, and its need to significantly improve its ability to provide basic services to the Afghan people.

The classified version of General McChrystal's report also provided his estimate of the personnel and resources that he believes would be required to execute his counterinsurgency strategy. These estimates have not been released in unclassified form, but numerous press reports indicate they include a variety of options requiring from 15,000 up to 80,000 additional troops to be deployed over the next year, with the number of troops deployed determining the extent of the areas that could be stabilized.

Over the past few months, President Obama convened nine meetings with the full range of his national security advisors, both civilian and military. The length of time taken to consider the strategy and resource options is indicative of the controversy within the Administration. It also reflects the acceptance that the security situation in Afghanistan is closely entwined with that of bordering areas of Pakistan, which both the Taliban and al-Qaeda cadres are using as staging and training areas, which consequently adds a significant level of complexity to the strategic considerations. Of fundamental importance to the Administration is establishing a timeline and process for turning over responsibility for security to the Afghan National Security Forces (ANSF).[9] There is, however, a certain tension between seeking to keep the U.S. military commitment from being open-ended and simultaneously seeking to assure both Afghan and international allies of a steadfast U.S. commitment.

While General McChrystal's assessments are based on undertaking a comprehensive counterinsurgency effort to stabilize Afghanistan, there are reportedly those in the Administration who believe that a more narrowly focused effort concentrating only on identifying and neutralizing terrorist cells and their facilities is a preferable course of action. They argue that this approach would require fewer resources and could achieve the fundamental goal of deterring further terrorist attacks on the United States and its allies originating from this region. Supporters of the more comprehensive counterinsurgency effort maintain that anything less will run the risk of the insurgency collapsing the Afghan government, resulting in the return of the Taliban ascendency and accommodation of al-Qaeda in Afghanistan and potentially increased instability in neighboring Pakistan.

[8] General Stanley McChrystal, "COMISAF's Initial Assessment," Headquarters, International Security Assistance Force, Kabul, Afghanistan. August 30, 2009 (Available at http://media.washingtonpost.com/wp-srv/politics/documents/Assessment_Redacted_092109.pdf

[9] Gerald Seib, "Exit Plan Critical to Afghan Build-up," *Wall Street Journal*, November 17, 2009.

President's December 1 Speech: The Way Forward in Afghanistan and Pakistan[10]

The President identified several objectives in Afghanistan and Pakistan: (1) disrupt, dismantle, and defeat al Qaeda; (2) deny al Qaeda a safe haven; (3) reverse the Taliban's momentum and deny it the ability to overthrow the government; and (4) strengthen the capacity of the Afghan security forces and government to better protect and serve population centers. To accomplish this, President Obama is ordering the deployment of an additional 30,000 troops to the region, which will bring the U.S. total to almost 100,000 troops. This deployment will be staged over the next six months, with the full additional complement being in-country by summer 2010. Noting that Afghan operations continue to be an international effort, President Obama expressed confidence that some of 42 coalition allies will also be increasing their contributions. NATO Secretary-General Rasmussen echoed this confidence, stating that he expects NATO allies to contribute at least an additional 5,000 troops in 2010.[11]

The President emphasized the importance of transferring lead responsibility for security to the ANSF by announcing his intent to start withdrawing U.S. forces from Afghanistan by July 2011. This element of the President's announcement has initially attracted the most attention in the press and in the Congress. Among the questions have been (1) whether this is intended to be a hard and fast deadline, or one subject to amendment; (2) given that the full 30,000 troop increase will not be completed before mid-2010, does that deadline provide sufficient time to achieve the U.S. objectives; (3) what criteria or "metrics" will be used to guide decisions on how fast to draw down; (4) whether a date-specific deadline for the start of a U.S. withdrawal will unsettle potential Afghan and Pakistani allies, causing them to question the steadfastness of the U.S. commitment in the region.

President Obama stressed that an effective partnership with the Pakistani government and military is an key element for the defeat of the Afghan insurgency, and that increased attention will be paid to strengthening this partnership through military and economic assistance.

The President's new Afghanistan strategy has received broad consideration within Congress, with multiple hearings being held by both the House and Senate Armed Services Committees, and the House Foreign Affairs and Senate Foreign Relations Committees.

Training Afghan Security Forces

In keeping with his intent to improve operational coordination, General McChrystal has consolidated the U.S. and NATO training mission under a single NATO command: National Training Mission—Afghanistan (NTM-A) It is hoped that this will encourage other NATO nations to increase their participation in the training effort There are currently about 94,000 personnel in the Afghan army and 91,000 police. NATO commanders hope to raise these numbers to 134,000 and 96,800 respectively by October 2010, with an eventual objective of a total of 400,000 Afghan National Security Forces.[12]

---

[10] Text of the President's speech is available at http://www.whitehouse.gov/the-press-office/remarks-president-address-nation-way-forward-afghanistan-and-pakistan

[11] "NATO Leader Expects Partners to Boost Contributions," *American Forces Press Service.* December 2, 2009.

[12] Jonathan Burch, "NATO Takes Command of the Afghan Army, Police Training," *Reuters*, November 21, 2009

Character of the War in Afghanistan

While war is always about the organized use of violence to achieve political ends, the character of a given war may change dramatically over time. Since 2001, the character of the war in Afghanistan has evolved markedly, from a violent struggle against al Qaeda and its Taliban supporters, to a multi-faceted counterinsurgency (COIN) effort.

In the aftermath of the terrorist attacks of September 11, 2001, the United States launched Operation Enduring Freedom (OEF) in order to end the ability of the Taliban regime to provide safe haven to al Qaeda and to put a stop to al Qaeda's use of the territory of Afghanistan as a base of operations for terrorist activities. In that first phase, a primarily military effort, U.S. and other coalition forces, working closely with Afghan opposition forces, quickly removed the Taliban regime.

After the fall of the Taliban, the character of the war shifted to a multifaceted COIN effort aimed at smothering the diffuse insurgency by shoring up the efforts of the government of the Islamic Republic of Afghanistan (GIRoA) to provide security, governance, and economic development. Leading practitioners view efforts in all three areas—and not just kinetic military operations—as essential to any successful counterinsurgency campaign. As U.S. Army General David Petraeus, now Commanding General of U.S. Central Command (CENTCOM), has frequently stated, "You can't kill your way out of an insurgency."[13] The three areas are generally viewed as interdependent and mutually-reinforcing—sufficient security is a prerequisite for some governance and development efforts, and longer-term, sustainable security requires both functional governance and economic opportunity. COIN theorists argue further that these areas require substantial civilian as well as military efforts. As the U.S. Army and Marine Corps 2006 COIN Manual states: "Military efforts are necessary and important to counterinsurgency efforts, but they are only effective when integrated into a comprehensive strategy employing all instruments of national power."[14]

As a central pillar of the COIN campaign in Afghanistan, the Afghan and international military effort aims broadly at defeating the remnants of the Taliban and other insurgents, securing the population, and helping extend the reach of the Afghan government. The international military effort now includes the North Atlantic Treaty Organization-led (NATO) International Security Assistance Force (ISAF), to which the U.S. government contributes troops, as well as the separate US-led OEF mission.

Prospects for the Outcome of the War

Afghanistan's results to date have been mixed, and no concrete end of the war is yet in sight. Despite the achievement of some major political milestones—including ratifying a new constitution and holding presidential and parliamentary elections—progress to date in extending the rule of law, establishing effective governance, and furthering economic development has been

---

[13] Babak Dehghanpisheh and Evan Thomas, "Scions of the Surge," *Newsweek*, March 24, 2008.

[14] Field Manual 3-24, *Counterinsurgency*, Headquarters, Department of the Army, December 2006, para. 2-1. Paragraph 2-2 of the COIN manual adds: "The integration of civilian and military efforts is crucial to successful COIN operations. All efforts focus on supporting the local populace and HN [host nation] government. Political, social, and economic programs are usually more valuable than conventional military operations in addressing the root causes of conflict and undermining an insurgency."

relatively limited, as reflected in the widespread corruption encountered in the Summer 2009 presidential elections. Meanwhile, for several years, practitioners and observers have expressed concerns about a worsening security situation on the ground, including the greater frequency and sophistication of attacks, exacerbated by the ability of insurgents to find safe haven across the border in Pakistan.

Experts differ on the further prospects for the Afghanistan effort and the war's likely outcome, in part because they pose the question in different ways. One approach addresses the relatively short-term goal of defeating the insurgency—that is, ensuring that insurgents cannot directly challenge the authority of the Afghan state.

As of late 2009, few if any practitioners or observers expected the war to end in a clear Taliban victory, including Taliban control of the state of Afghanistan. Some suggested that a more likely worst-case scenario would be a reversion to the civil war and chaos of the early 1990s, including warlordism, a general lack of stability and opportunity for ordinary Afghans, and a proliferation of ungoverned spaces that might be used by terrorists as safe havens. To some extent, these conditions are currently manifested in parts of southern Afghanistan.

In late 2008, as a rule, U.S. and other international senior officials in Afghanistan expressed measured optimism regarding near-term results of the counterinsurgency effort. They pointed to some recent progress breaking down insurgent networks and expected further gains, particularly if more resources were made available and greater cooperation from all parties, including neighboring states, achieved. As a rule, international officials did not argue that without more resources, the COIN effort would fail, but rather, that without more resources, the effort would cost more money, more time, and more lives.[15] In August 2009, General Mc Chrystal's report carried a notably less optimistic assessment, raising the possibility of failure without timely and adequate resourcing of the allied counterinsurgency efforts.

Another approach to the question of Afghanistan's prospects takes a broader and longer-term view. Observers from this school of thought point to thirty years of war, occupation, displacement and chaos that have destroyed Afghanistan's infrastructure, ravaged its human capital resources, and left most of its relatively youthful population with no memories of living in a society not disrupted by conflict. Some experts caution that even if the insurgency is defeated in the near-term, it is not hard to imagine that some remnants or some later generations might draw inspiration from the current fight, and resume the attack whenever the political and security constellation seems more conducive to their success—as Afghans say, "You have the watches; we have the time." Other observers note that in comparative and historical global perspective, it is quite rare for states to achieve "stability" and "good governance," and that Afghanistan, given its relative poverty of human and natural resources, faces steep challenges and unlikely odds in aiming at those objectives. Accordingly, some senior U.S. and other international officials have urged a tempering of expectations about Afghanistan's long-term prospects.

---

[15] In November 2008, International Security Assistance Force Commanding General, U.S. Army General David McKiernan noted that without additional resources, it would be "a longer fight with greater sacrifices." General David McKiernan, Interview, Kabul, Afghanistan, November 2008.

Purpose of This Report

This report provides a examination of the war's background, context, and early execution; an analytical discussion of the COIN war to date, including strategy, organization, participation, and key facets of the effort including population security, advising the Afghan National Security Forces (ANSF), counter-narcotics, reconciliation, community outreach, and civil-military coordination; and an analysis of major strategic and operational issues and options that the 111th Congress may opt to consider.

Background: Context and Early History of the War

Current efforts to support security, governance and development in Afghanistan take place in the aftermath of thirty grueling years of conflict and unrest, followed by OEF military operations that removed the Taliban regime and the rapid creation of a new, post-Taliban political order.

Prelude to War[16]

In December 1979, the Soviet Union invaded Afghanistan to shore up a puppet communist regime. During the 1980's, armed Afghan resistance groups known as "mujahedin" waged war against Soviet forces and the Afghan security forces that supported them.[17] During that period, the U.S. government, through the Central Intelligence Agency (CIA), provided covert assistance to mujahedin groups, working through Pakistan's Inter-Services Intelligence Directorate (ISI).

In 1989, Soviet forces withdrew from Afghanistan, and in April 1992, the Soviet-backed Afghan regime in Kabul fell to mujahedin forces, which established a form of rule including a rotating presidency. In November 1994, the ethnically Pashtun-dominated Taliban movement led by Mullah Omar seized the city of Kandahar, in southern Afghanistan.[18] In 1996, the Taliban captured Kabul and retained control over much of the country until ousted by OEF operations in 2001. However, throughout its tenure, the Taliban continued to face armed opposition, in particular from the Northern Alliance, a loose network dominated by ethnic Tajiks and Uzbeks, primarily from northern Afghanistan. Key legacies of Afghanistan's years of civil war, conflict, and oppressive rule included the deaths of over a million people, the displacement of millions more, the proliferation of available weapons, and the destruction of key institutions and infrastructure.

---

[16] For background see Steve Coll, *Ghost Wars: The Secret History of the CIA, Afghanistan, and Bin Laden, from the Soviet Invasion to September 10, 2001* (New York: Penguin, 2004); George Crile, *Charlie Wilson's War: The Extraordinary Story of How the Wildest Man in Congress and a Rogue CIA Agent Changed the History of our Times* (New York: Grove Press, 2003); Robert D. Kaplan, *Soldiers of God: With Islamic Warriors in Afghanistan and Pakistan* (New York: Vintage Departures, 2001); and Ahmed Rashid, *Taliban: Militant Islam, Oil and Fundamentalism in Central Asia* (New Haven, CT: Yale University Press, 2001).

[17] The plural noun "mujahedin" (singular "mujahid"), borrowed from Arabic and now used in standard English, refers to a group of Muslims waging "jihad," or "a holy war waged on behalf of Islam as a religious duty." See "jihad," Merriam-Webster Online Dictionary 2008, Merriam-Webster online, available at http://www.merriam-webster.com/dictionary/jihad; and "mujahideen," *Merriam-Webster Online Dictionary 2008*, Merriam-Webster online, available at http://www.merriam-webster.com/dictionary/mujahideen>.

[18] The term "Taliban," in Pashto, is the plural of "talib" (student), which is derived from Arabic. See "Taliban," *Merriam-Webster Online Dictionary 2008*, Merriam-Webster online, available at http://www.merriam-webster.com/dictionary/Taliban.

The proximate cause of U.S. military operations in Afghanistan was the linkage of the September 11, 2001, terrorist attacks to al Qaeda, which trained and operated under Taliban protection in Afghanistan. In an address to a joint session of Congress on September 20, 2001, President George W. Bush stated U.S. demands on the Taliban, warning: "The Taliban must act, and act immediately. They will hand over the terrorists or they will share in their fate."[19]

Major Combat Operations

On October 7, 2001, following the refusal of the Taliban regime to cease harboring al Qaeda, the U.S. government launched military operations in Afghanistan, with the stated purpose of disrupting the use of Afghanistan as a terrorist base of operations and attacking the military capability of the Taliban regime.[20]

In contrast to the lengthy, iterative preparations that preceded the launch of Operation Iraqi Freedom, the U.S. planning process for OEF was extremely condensed. The concept of operations was based on Secretary of Defense Donald Rumsfeld's vision of defense transformation, including the idea that a heavier reliance on cutting-edge technology and precision weaponry could make possible the deployment of smaller-sized conventional ground forces.

Military operations were preceded and complemented by work by the Central Intelligence Agency (CIA) with Afghan opposition groups on the ground. Initial U.S. operations relied on the use of special operations forces (SOF) on the ground, enabled by air assets, working by, with and through indigenous partners, in particular the Northern Alliance. Many U.S. defense experts regarded the operations as an important demonstration of operational "jointness"—the ability of Military Services to work together seamlessly. The United Kingdom and Australia also deployed forces to support the major combat phase of operations, and dozens of other countries provided basing, access and overflight permission.[21]

---

[19] The full list of demands included "Deliver to United States authorities all of the leaders of Al Qaeda who hide in your land. Release all foreign nationals, including American citizens you have unjustly imprisoned. Protect foreign journalists, diplomats and aid workers in your country. Close immediately and permanently every terrorist training camp in Afghanistan, and hand over every terrorist and every person and their support structure to appropriate authorities. Give the United States full access to terrorist training camps, so we can make sure they are no longer operating." See President George W. Bush, Address to Joint Session of Congress, September 20, 2001, available at http://www.whitehouse.gov/news/releases/2001/09/20010920-8.html.

[20] See Statement by President George W. Bush, October 7, 2001, available at http://www.whitehouse.gov/news/releases/2001/10/20011007-8.html. Many observers consider that at the launch of OEF, short-term U.S. objectives – including targeting al Qaeda – together with the means to achieve them, were much more clearly articulated than any longer-term U.S. vision for Afghanistan's future, together with the approaches necessary to achieve that vision.

[21] The United Kingdom's publicly stated campaign objectives included bringing Osama bin Laden and other al Qaeda leaders to justice; preventing them from posing a further terrorist threat; and ensuring that Afghanistan ceased to harbor terrorists; in pursuit of the broader objective to "do everything possible to eliminate the threat posed by international terrorism." See Ministry of Defence, United Kingdom, "Defeating International Terrorism: Campaign Objectives," October 16, 2001, available at http://www.mod.uk. For a detailed discussion of the March 2002 Operation Anaconda, which included SOF and conventional forces, coalition partners, and Afghan forces, see Sean Naylor, *Not a Good Day to Die: The Untold Story of Operation Anaconda* (New York: Berkley Books, 2005). For an analysis of the lessons of Afghanistan operations for future warfighting, see Stephen Biddle, Afghanistan and the Future of Warfare: Implications for Army and Defense Policy, Carlisle, PA: Strategic Studies Institute, November 2002.

Military victory, including the demise of the Taliban regime, came quickly. In November 2001, the Taliban fled Kabul, and in December they left their stronghold, the southern city of Kandahar. It is generally understood that in December 2001, key al Qaeda and Taliban leaders fled across the border into Pakistan.

To fill the political void, in December 2001, in Bonn, Germany, the United Nations hosted the so-called Bonn Conference. Participants included representatives of four Afghan opposition groupings, and observers included representatives of neighboring and other key countries including the United States. The resulting Bonn Agreement created an Afghan Interim Authority to serve as the "repository of Afghan sovereignty" and outlined a political process for producing a new constitution and choosing a new Afghan government. In contrast to the model pursued in Iraq from 2003 to 2004, in Afghanistan there was no period of formal occupation in which an international authority exercised sovereignty on behalf of the Afghans.[22] To help provide security to support the fledgling new regime, in December 2001 the United Nations authorized an international force—the International Security Assistance Force (ISAF)—with a mandate to help the Afghans maintain security in Kabul and surrounding areas. The United Kingdom agreed to lead the force initially.[23]

The major combat operations phase was regarded as a quick success by its Afghan protagonists and their U.S. and other international partners, but the challenges were far from over. The new Afghan leadership faced the profound political challenge of consolidating a fractious, scarred state, with very few resources. The new leaders also faced potential violent challenges, both from resurgent al Qaeda and Taliban leaders who were defeated but not eliminated, and from Afghan local power-brokers, strengthened by years of battle-hardened autonomy and resistance, who were displeased by the emerging post-Taliban order.

Counterinsurgency War in Afghanistan to Date

Both the security climate—including the composition, strategy, and tactics of the insurgency—and the structure and focus of international efforts designed to support the Afghan government have changed substantially since the end of the major combat operations that ousted the Taliban regime. This section describes and analyzes key developments in the counterinsurgency war in Afghanistan with an emphasis on recent trends and initiatives.

Strategy

In 2008, as international interest in, and attention to, the war in Afghanistan grew, a number of observers stressed the need for clearer or more robust strategy to guide Afghan and international efforts. "Strategy" is commonly understood to include a statement of objectives, or desired ends;

---

[22] In accordance with the provisions of the Bonn Agreement, a large meeting – a "loya jirga" – was held in June 2002, at which Hamid Karzai was elected head of the new Afghan Transitional Authority. A new constitution was adopted in January 2004; presidential elections, in which Karzai was elected, were held in October 2004; and National Assembly elections were held in September 2005. See the *Agreement on Provisional Arrangements in Afghanistan Pending the Re-Establishment of Permanent Government Institutions,* Bonn, December 5, 2001, available at http://www.mfa.gov.af/Documents/ImportantDoc/The%20Bonn%20Agreement.pdf.

[23] See S/RES/1386 (2001), December 20, 2001. The UK was followed by Turkey, and then Germany, see S/RES/1413 (2002), May 23, 2002, and S/RES/1444 (2002), November 27, 2002.

---

the ways and means designed to achieve those ends; and the roles and responsibilities of key players in executing those ways and means.[24]

Strategy-making for Afghanistan is particularly complicated, for two main reasons. First, the range of strategic objectives is quite broad, encompassing not only security progress but also, for example, civilian capacity-building, the rule of law, counternarcotics, and economic development. Those fields, in turn, are closely linked empirically—for example, long-term development requires a relatively stable environment, and successful counternarcotics efforts must be predicated on some form of rule of law. Second, strategy-making is complicated by the range of actors providing some support to GIRoA, including NATO, the United Nations, and other international organizations, as well as individual states, each of which may have its own—or even competing sets of—interests and priorities. Military strategy, in turn, is not easily separable from broader grand strategy for Afghanistan, since security is essential for progress in other areas, and since military forces play key supporting roles in the non-security lines of operation.

NATO Strategy

At its 20th Summit, held in Bucharest, Romania, in April 2008, NATO issued a streamlined but clear strategic vision for Afghanistan. That vision established four "guiding principles": a firm and shared long-term commitment; support for enhanced Afghan leadership and responsibility; a comprehensive approach by the international community, bringing together civilian and military efforts; and increased cooperation and engagement with Afghanistan's neighbors, especially Pakistan. The document also included a "vision of success," which is essentially a statement of objectives: "extremism and terrorism will no longer pose a threat to stability; Afghan National Security Forces will be in the lead and self-sufficient; and the Afghan government will be able to extend the reach of good governance, reconstruction, and development throughout the country to the benefit of all its citizens."[25] What the "strategic vision" did not provide in any detail was a clear articulation of the specific ways and means ISAF would use to achieve those objectives.

Arguably closing the strategy gap substantially, ISAF, in October 2008, issued a classified Joint Campaign Plan (JCP). The JCP was General McKiernan's guidance to the force, and it specified key assumptions, objectives, and approaches to be used to achieve those objectives. It stated that the primary goal is the "transfer of lead security responsibility" to the Afghans, which includes planning as well as conducting operations. The JCP addressed all the lines of operation (LOO) discussed in the Afghanistan Compact but underscored that NATO has the lead only for the security LOO. Importantly, the JCP framed ISAF's mission in counterinsurgency (COIN) terms— the mission includes defeating an "insurgency" and the basic approach follows the COIN logic of "shape, clear, hold, build." ISAF officials considered the use of COIN terminology a breakthrough, following years of NATO preference for framing the effort in Afghanistan in terms of stability operations.[26]

---

[24] It is a fundamental principle of military theory that war is driven by political goals of one kind or another. The Prussian writer Carl von Clausewitz argued that policy "…will permeate all military operations, and, in so far as their violent nature will admit, it will have a continuous influence on them." Carl von Clausewitz, *On War,* translated by Michael Howard and Peter Paret (Princeton, NJ: Princeton University Press, 1976.)

[25] "Strategic Vision," NATO, available at http://www.nato.int/docu/pr/2008/p08-052e.html.

[26] ISAF officials, Interviews, Kabul, Afghanistan, November 2008.

In October 2009, NATO Defense Ministers met in Bratislava and adopted four priorities for ISAF operations: (1) focus upon the Afghan population; (2) enhanced efforts to build the capacity of the Afghan National Security Forces; (3) promote better Afghan governance; (4) to engage more effectively with Afghanistan's neighbors, particularly Pakistan.[27]

U.S. Government Strategy

The U.S. government plays a significant leadership role in both ISAF and NATO as a whole, and thus helps shape NATO and ISAF strategy and approaches. At the same time, the United States may have national interests in Afghanistan and the region that are not shared by all ISAF contributors, and the relative priority of various interests may differ among the Allies.

The U.S. government has not published a formal strategy for Afghanistan, along the lines of the November 2005 *National Strategy for Victory in Iraq*.[28] Key Obama Administration officials have nevertheless outlined several elements of the U.S. strategy. Under Secretary of Defense for Policy, Michèle Flournoy has stated that "our strategic objective is a stable and secure Afghanistan in which al Qaeda and the network of insurgent groups, including the Taliban, are incapable of seriously threatening the Afghan state and resurrecting a safe haven for terrorism."[29] Secretary of State Hillary Clinton has indicated that President Obama's Afghanistan strategy focuses on these elements: sending additional troops to Afghanistan; providing a "major increase" in non-military aid to Afghanistan; confronting the drug trade; and developing a coherent Pakistan policy. Furthermore, based on a policy of "more for more," aid to GIRoA would be tied to better performance.[30]

CENTCOM conducted a 100-day comprehensive strategic review of its entire area of responsibility, including Afghanistan. For his part, General McKiernan, then ISAF Commander, suggested that U.S. interests might include ensuring that Afghanistan cannot harbor terrorists; establishing a controlled Afghanistan/ Pakistan border; promoting a degree of regional stability; supporting a constructive role for Iran; and encouraging some form of freedom and democracy for the Afghan people.[31]

Upon assuming office, President Obama initiated an interagency policy review and consultations with both coalition allies and the governments of both Afghanistan and Pakistan. On March 27, 2009, President Obama outlined a strategy for continuing operations in both Afghanistan and Pakistan based on this review, which included consultations with coalition allied governments and those of Afghanistan and Pakistan. The white paper summarizing the review report listed five objectives:[32]

---

[27] NATO press release, "NATO Ministers agree on key priorities for Afghanistan," October 23, 2009.

[28] National Security Council, *National Strategy for Victory in Iraq,* November 2005, available at http://www.whitehouse.gov/infocus/iraq/iraq_strategy_nov2005.html.

[29] See replies to questions for the record, submitted by Under Secretary of Defense for Policy nominee to the Senate Armed Services Committee (SASC), for her January 15, 2009, confirmation hearing, available at http://armed-services.senate.gov/statemnt/2009/January/Flournoy%2001-15-09.pdf.

[30] See the replies to questions for the record, submitted by Secretary of State nominee Hillary Clinton to the Senate Foreign Relations Committee (SFRC), for her January 13, 2009, confirmation hearing, available at http://www.foreignpolicy.com/files/KerryClintonQFRs.pdf.

[31] General David McKiernan, Interview, Kabul, Afghanistan, November 2008.

[32] Interagency Policy Group, *White Paper of the Interagency Policy Group's report on U.S. Policy toward Afghanistan* (continued...)

- Disrupting terrorist networks in Afghanistan and especially Pakistan to degrade any ability to plan and launch international terrorist attacks.

- Promoting a more capable, accountable, and effective government in Afghanistan.

- Developing increasingly self-reliant Afghan security forces that can lead the counterinsurgency and counterterrorism fight with reduced U.S. assistance.

- Assisting efforts to enhance civilian control and stable constitutional government in Pakistan and a vibrant Pakistani economy.

- Involving the international community to actively assist in addressing these objectives for Afghanistan and Pakistan, with an important leadership role for the United Nations.

The white paper defined two priority missions for U.S. military forces in Afghanistan: (1) to secure Afghanistan's south and east regions against a return of al Qaeda and its allies, and provide a space for the Afghan government to establish effective control, and (2) to provide Afghan security forces the mentoring required to expand rapidly and take the lead in counterinsurgency operations, thereby allowing U.S. forces to "wind down" combat operations.[33] To carry out these missions, the Administration's review called for "executing and resourcing an integrated civilian-military counterinsurgency strategy."

In June, 2009 General Stanley McChrystal assumed command of U.S.-NATO forces in Afghanistan and undertook another review of the security situation in Afghanistan, resulting a report submitted to the Department of Defense in August 2009. General McChrystal particularly emphasized (1) a comprehensive counterinsurgency strategy focused on the welfare of the Afghan population; (2) improving ISAF's unity of effort and command; (3) increasing the size and capability of Afghan security forces and operational "partnering" with allied forces; (4) improving Afghan civil governance and reducing governmental corruption; (5) gaining the initiative against the insurgency throughout the country; and (6) prioritizing allocation of resources to the most threatened populations.[34]

In response to General McChrystal's report, and the tenuous political situation in Afghanistan in the wake of the flawed presidential election there, the Obama Administration undertook the most extensive review yet of strategy regarding Afghanistan. The review's conclusions, outlined in President Obama's December 3 speech at the U.S. Military Academy, essentially endorsed the principals of the March white paper. The President's decision to augment U.S. forces in Afghanistan with an additional 30,000 troops reflected a desire to accelerate the three main military elements of the strategy: (1) break the momentum of the insurgency, (2) better secure the major population centers, and (3) increase the number and improve the performance of Afghan National Security Forces. The President also announced that the increased U.S. force level

---

(...continued)

and Pakistan, Office of the President, Washington, DC, March 2009, pp. 1-5, http://www.whitehouse.gov/assets/documents/Afghanistan-Pakistan_White_Paper.pdf.

[33] Ibid., p. 2

[34] General Stanley McChrystal, "COMISAF's Initial Assessment," Headquarters, International Security Assistance Force, Kabul, Afghanistan. August 30, 2009 (available at http://media.washingtonpost.com/wp-srv/politics/documents/Assessment_Redacted_092109.pdf.

(approximately 98,000 troops) would be maintained until July 2011, at which time a withdrawal of U.S. forces would begin. The pace and size of the withdrawal will be dependent upon the state of the security environment at that time.

International Efforts: Organization and Coordination

Afghanistan, which lacks sufficient institutional, material and human resources to make substantial progress on its own, relies deeply on the international community to support the three main pillars of the counterinsurgency effort: security, governance and development. However, most practitioners and observers contend that ever since the Bonn Conference, the multi-faceted international effort has suffered from a dearth of resources in each area, and from insufficient coordination among key players and their initiatives. This assessment was reinforced by General McChrystal's August 2009 report.

The "lead nation" model of international assistance to Afghanistan was agreed to at a donors' conference held in Tokyo in early 2002. Five countries each agreed to assume lead coordination responsibility for assistance to a single area of security-related Afghan administration: the United States for the army, Germany for the police, Italy for the judiciary, the United Kingdom for counternarcotics, and Japan for the disarmament, demobilization and reintegration (DDR) of militias.

The Afghanistan Compact, a formal statement of commitment by the government of the Islamic Republic of Afghanistan (GIRoA) and the international community, finalized in January 2006, shifted responsibility from lead nations to Afghanistan itself. The premise was a shared Afghan and international vision of Afghanistan's future, including the commitment of the international community to "provide resources and support" to realize that vision. The Compact established three broad pillars of activity for future efforts—security; governance, the rule of law and human rights; and economic and social development. To "ensure overall strategic coordination of the implementation of the Compact," the document established the Joint Coordination and Monitoring Board (JCMB), co-chaired by a GIRoA representative and the United Nations Special Representative of the Secretary-General (UN SRSG).[35]

The UN SRSG leads the United Nations Assistance Mission in Afghanistan (UNAMA), which was established by the UN Security Council in early 2002.[36] The current UNAMA mandate confirms the UN SRSG's lead coordination role, as described by the Afghanistan Compact, but clarifies that the UN plays a stronger coordination role vis-à-vis civilian assistance efforts, than for military ones. The mandate states that the UN SRSG will "lead the international civilian efforts" to promote "...more coherent support by the international community to the Afghan Government." Concerning military efforts, the UN SRSG will work to "strengthen cooperation with ISAF at all levels."[37]

---

[35] See *The Afghanistan Compact: Building on Success*, London Conference on Afghanistan, London, January 31-February 1, 2006, available at http://www.nato.int/isaf/docu/epub/pdf/afghanistan_compact.pdf.

[36] See S/RES/1401 (2002), March 28, 2002. The mandate is renewed annually.

[37] See S/RES/1806 (2008), March 20, 2008, which extended the mandate of UNAMA for one year.

Security Line of Operation: Organization

International military forces in Afghanistan lead support to GIRoA in the field of security—one of the three pillars of the Afghanistan Compact—and support international civilian initiatives in the other two fields, governance and development. Over time, the mandates, structure and composition of the international force presence in Afghanistan have changed significantly, as the role of NATO has increased and the character of the fight has evolved. Today, NATO leads the International Security Assistance Force (ISAF), and the United States leads the OEF coalition effort. The U.S. government contributes troops to both missions. The command of these two efforts has now been unified under U.S. Army General Stanley McChrystal.

NATO International Security Assistance Force (ISAF)[38]

ISAF represents NATO's first significant out-of-area deployment, and it is viewed by many observers as a key test for the Alliance—a measure of both its current capabilities and its possible future relevance. On September 12, 2001, in response to the 9/11 terrorist attacks, NATO for the first time invoked Article 5 of the North Atlantic Treaty, which confirms the commitment of the allies to collective self-defense in the event of armed attack on any party to the treaty.[39] That action helped clear the way for future NATO operations in Afghanistan. On August 9, 2003, NATO assumed responsibility for the ISAF mission, which had been established by UN mandate in December 2001 and led until mid-2003 by a series of lead nations.

ISAF Stages

ISAF, initially mandated to support Afghan efforts to secure Kabul and its immediate environs, expanded its geographical scope in four stages. During Stage 1, completed on October 1, 2004, ISAF expanded to the north of Kabul, assuming responsibility for a German-led Provincial Reconstruction Team (PRT) and establishing new PRTs. In Stage 2, completed in September 2005, ISAF expanded to the west. In Stage 3, completed on July 31, 2006, ISAF assumed responsibility for southern Afghanistan. In Stage 4, completed on October 5, 2006, ISAF assumed control of U.S.-led forces in eastern Afghanistan.[40]

ISAF Mandate

The focus of ISAF efforts has been a source of contention among the Allies, many of whom agreed to contribute troops on the premise that ISAF's focus would be post-conflict stability operations. That premise may have been valid at the time of ISAF's formation, but by several years later, the security climate had changed and an organized, capable insurgency had emerged. ISAF Commanding General, U.S. Army General David McKiernan, stated in November 2008: "The fact is that we are at war in Afghanistan. It's not peacekeeping. It's not stability operations.

---

[38] For further background, including the perspectives of key ISAF troop contributors, see CRS Report RL33627, *NATO in Afghanistan: A Test of the Transatlantic Alliance*, by Vincent Morelli and Paul Belkin.

[39] See Article 5, *The North Atlantic Treaty*, signed April 4, 1949, Washington, DC, available at http://www.nato.int/docu/basictxt/treaty.htm.

[40] See International Security Assistance Force "Placemat," dated December 1, 2008, available at http://www.nato.int/isaf/docu/epub/pdf/isaf_placemat_081201.pdf.

It's not humanitarian assistance. It's war."[41] ISAF's mission statement reflects the insurgency challenge: "ISAF conducts operations in partnership with GIRoA and in coordination with OEF, UNAMA, and the international community in order to assist GIRoA to defeat the insurgency, establish a secure environment, extend viable governance, and promote development throughout Afghanistan."[42]

ISAF Phases

From the outset, NATO planned that ISAF operations in Afghanistan would have four phases. The first phase was "assessment and preparation," including initial operations only in Kabul. The second phase was ISAF's geographic expansion throughout Afghanistan, completed in 2006. The final three phases would be stabilization; transition; and redeployment. At the start of 2009, ISAF was operating in Phase III, "stabilization," and NATO officials were reportedly discussing when to announce the commencement of Phase IV, the "transition" of lead security responsibility to the Afghan National Security Forces (ANSF). Some ISAF officials have expressed the concern that an announcement that ISAF has entered "transition" could trigger a rush by some troop-contributing countries to Phase V—"redeployment." They caution that in practice, the shift from stabilization to transition is likely to vary geographically across Afghanistan as the abilities of various ANSF to execute and then lead missions increase, and to take place in fits and starts, rather than at a clear single point in time.[43]

ISAF Organization

ISAF is led by a four-star combined headquarters, based in Kabul and headed by U.S. Army General Stanley McChrystal. NATO's North Atlantic Council provides political direction for the mission. NATO's Supreme Headquarters Allied Powers in Europe (SHAPE), based in Mons, Belgium, and led by Supreme Allied Commander Europe (SACEUR), U.S. Navy Admiral James Stavridis, provides strategic command and control. NATO's Joint Force Command Headquarters, which is based in Brunssum, The Netherlands, and reports to SHAPE, provides "overall operational control," including many administrative responsibilities. ISAF itself, which reports to SHAPE through Joint Forces Command, exercises "in-theater operational command." This arrangement, including two levels of operational headquarters, is somewhat unusual.

In Afghanistan, ISAF oversees five contiguous Regional Commands (RC), each led by a two-star general: RC-Center, led by France; RC-North, led by Germany; RC-West, led by Italy; RC-South, under rotating lead by Canada, the Netherlands, and the United Kingdom; and RC-East, led by the United States. Troop contingents from other Allies, and from some non-NATO partners, serve under these Regional Commands.

---

[41] General David McKiernan, Atlantic Council, Washington, DC, November 18, 2008, transcript available at http://www.acus.org/event_blog/general-david-d-mckiernan-speaks-councils-commanders-series/transcript.

[42] Interviews with ISAF officials, Kabul, Afghanistan, November 2008.

[43] Interviews with ISAF officials, Kabul, Afghanistan, November 2008.

ISAF Troop Contributions

As of February 1, 2010, ISAF included 85,795 from 43 countries, including NATO Allies and non-NATO partners.[44]

	Country	#		Country	#		Country	#
	Albania	255		Georgia	175		Portugal	105
	Armenia	0		Germany	4415		Romania	945
	Australia	1550		Greece	15		Singapore	40
	Austria	2		Hungary	315		Slovakia	240
	Azerbaijan	90		Iceland	3		Slovenia	70
	Belgium	575		Ireland	8		Spain	1070
	Bosnia & Herzegovina	10		Italy	3150		Sweden	410
	Bulgaria	540		Jordan	0		The Former Yugoslav Republic of Macedonia¹	165
	Canada	2830		Latvia	175		Turkey	1755
	Croatia	295		Lithuania	165		Ukraine	8
	Czech Republic	440		Luxembourg	9		United Arab Emirates	25
	Denmark	750		Netherlands	1940		United Kingdom	9500
	Estonia	150		New Zealand	220		United States	47085
	Finland	95		Norway	500			
	France	3750		Poland	1955		Total	85795

NATO Secretary-General Rasmussen, following a meeting of foreign ministers in December 2009, said he expected additional pledges of at least 5,000 troops to be forthcoming. Since then, a number of new NATO pledges not reflected in the above table have been announced: Albania, 125; Croatia, 40; Czech Republic, 100; Germany, 500; Italy, 1,040; Lithuania, 20; Poland, 680; Portugal, 120; Romania, 700; Slovakia, 240; Spain, 500; Turkey (N/A); United Kingdom, 1,200. Non-NATO nations that have made additional commitments are Armenia, 40; Australia, 120; Finland, 25; Georgia, 923; Macedonia, 80; Sweden, 125; Ukraine, 22. Other nations that have indicated possible contributions are Colombia, Kazakhstan, Mongolia, Montenegro, and South Korea. At the same time, however, Canada and the Netherlands will be withdrawing their contingents in 2011 and 2010, respectively.[45]

From the outset, NATO has struggled to secure sufficient troop contributions for ISAF. One consideration for potential troop contributors is cost—NATO's long-standing practice, "costs lie where they fall," typically means that countries pay their own costs when they contribute troops to a mission such as Afghanistan. Another consideration is the need for domestic political support.

---

[44] International Security Assistance Force "Placemat" dated October 22, 2009, available at http://www.nato.int/isaf/docu/epub/pdf/placemat.pdf.

[45] Erlanger, Steven. "Europe's Revolving Door in Afghanistan," *New York Times*, December 21, 2009.

ISAF National Caveats

From the outset, ISAF operations have been constrained by "national caveats"—restrictions that individual troop-contributing countries impose on their own forces' activities. Caveats tend to be informed by domestic political constraints—a government may consider, for example, that only by limiting its troops' activities, and hedging against taking casualties, can it guard against strong popular domestic opposition to its troop contribution. As a rule, troop-contributing countries state their caveats explicitly; but additional constraints may surface when unanticipated requirements arise and contingents seek additional guidance from their capitals.

The nature and extent of national caveats varies greatly among ISAF participants. Senior U.S. military officials point with concern, for example, to constraints on German forces in Afghanistan, which are imposed by Germany's parliament the Bundestag. These include restrictions on German training and advisory teams that do not allow them to conduct combined offensive operations with their Afghan counterparts, and on capable German Special Operations Forces (SOF) that are "FOB-locked," that is, effectively confined to their Forward Operating Base. Not all contingents are so constrained. U.S. officials praise, for example, the 700-strong French infantry battalion that works closely with U.S. SOF and Afghan counterparts in Kapisa province, at the "north gate" into Kabul, which witnessed growing insurgent infiltration in 2008.

National caveats frustrate commanders on the ground because they inhibit commanders' freedom to apportion forces across the battlespace—to move and utilize forces freely. With caveats, the "whole" of the international force, as some observers have suggested, is less than the sum of its parts. Even more damaging, ISAF officials note, is the impact caveats can have on ISAF's relationship with Afghan National Security Forces (ANSF) counterparts. For example, ISAF advisory teams that are unable to accompany ANSF counterparts on offensive operations quickly lose both the Afghans' respect, and their own ability to shape and mentor the Afghan forces. Afghan Minister of Defense Abdul Rahim Wardak stated that ISAF training teams "don't have the same quality" as their U.S. counterparts.[46] U.S. senior military officials in Afghanistan frequently note that the ANSF appreciate their U.S. counterparts because "we drink from the same canteen."[47] The U.S. government has consistently urged ISAF troop contributors to drop or ease their national caveats, with some limited success.

Coordination Within NATO/ISAF

ISAF officials note that both command and control, and coordination, within the NATO mission in Afghanistan leave some room for improvement.

One challenge is ensuring a full command relationship between ISAF headquarters and the Regional Commands. In RC-South, for example, the major troop contributors—the UK, Canada, the Netherlands—are strong partners relatively unconstrained by caveats. But ISAF officials note that RC-South effectively includes four provincially-based national campaigns—Dutch, British, Canadian, and U.S.—based on the provinces in which their respective troops are deployed. Each of these ISAF countries, in turn, tends to lobby the relevant Afghan Ministers in Kabul for

---

[46] Minister of Defense of Afghanistan Abdul Rahim Wardak, Interview, Kabul, Afghanistan, November 2008.

[47] General David McKiernan and other U.S. officials, Interviews, Kabul, Afghanistan, November 2008. One additional consequence of national caveats is a tendency for U.S. troops in Afghanistan to regard ISAF with a degree of humorous skepticism – "ISAF," the line goes, stands for "I Stop At Four," or alternatively, "I Saw Americans Fighting."

assistance to "its" province. The RC-South commander, ISAF officials underscore, has never been empowered to give comprehensive guidance to the other nations in that RC command. In November 2008, the new RC-South Commanding General, Major General de Kruif from the Netherlands, indicated the relatively low standard of expectations, stating: "it's not about unity of command, but about unity of effort."[48] As have his predecessors, General McChrystal has stressed, however, that a more closely integrated effort is necessary, not least because insurgents and tribes do not define their efforts by provincial or district boundaries.[49]

An additional challenge is information flow among ISAF participants. Senior U.S. officials at the ISAF HQ in Kabul note that they have a much clearer operational picture of eastern and southern Afghanistan, where most U.S. forces operate, than of northern and western Afghanistan. Constraints on information flow may include the use of different—national and NATO—communications channels, linguistic barriers, and some reluctance on the part of some countries to share information perceived to be especially sensitive.

In August 2009, the NATO nations approved a new ISAF command structure to reflect a mission expanded since ISAF's inception in both scope and geographical area. In the new structure, the ISAF Commander (COMISAF), a four-star slot, will also be dual-hatted as commander of U.S. forces participating in Operation Enduring Freedom. COMISAF will also focus on strategic political-military mission aspects, coordinating ISAF operations with Afghan security forces and other international organizations. COMISAF will also oversee the NATO training mission and the special operations forces operating in Afghanistan. A new three-star position, ISAF Joint Commander (COMICJ) will be responsible for the full range of daily tactical operations, overseeing the five regional commands and the Provincial Reconstruction Teams.

Another major challenge is maintaining situational awareness of—let alone control over—the activities of the 26 nationally-sponsored Provincial Reconstruction Teams (PRTs), which foster the ability of Afghan provincial-level officials to provide and promote governance, development and security. Officially, the military component of each PRT falls under ISAF command.[50] In practice, despite an ISAF directive that the PRT military components must report to ISAF on their activities, information flow has been spotty. One senior ISAF official speculated that one reason for the historical failure to comply might have been the perception that such efforts were wasted—that is, that the ISAF HQ made little use of such data and provided nothing back to the PRTs in return. The lack of a clear, shared picture of PRT activities has frustrated not only the ISAF leadership, but also Afghan and UN officials, in their efforts to apply resources strategically and effectively.[51]

In November 2008, the ISAF HQ restructured PRT oversight, to include the capability to share lessons learned and provide analytical feedback to PRTs. And in December 2008, a long-moribund Executive Steering Committee, including senior leadership from ISAF, GIRoA, and UNAMA, was reconstituted. As a result, the information flow concerning PRTs has improved.

---

[48] Major General de Kruif, Interview, Kandahar, Afghanistan, November 2008.

[49] General David McKiernan, Interview, Kabul, Afghanistan, November 2008.

[50] PRTs are variously civilian- or military-led, and may include any combination of civilian and military personnel, see below.

[51] Interviews with ISAF officials, Kabul, Afghanistan, November 2008. The March 2008 Report of the UN Secretary-General stressed the role of UNAMA in addressing "how to harmonize the activities of the provincial reconstruction teams." See A/62/722-S/2008/159, *The situation in Afghanistan and its implications for international peace and security, Report of the Secretary-General*, March 6, 2008.

One further challenge to full ISAF unity of command is the distinct mandate and role of the NATO Senior Civilian Representative (SCR), a position held since July 2008 by Italian Ambassador Fernando Gentilini. The SCR is the representative in Afghanistan of the NATO Secretary-General and reports regularly to the North Atlantic Council. As described by Ambassador Gentilini, the purpose is to "show that NATO is not just a military organization but that it can contribute to the political process more broadly."[52] Some ISAF senior officials view the SCR position—not necessarily any specific incumbent—as a "free agent," since the SCR is not part of ISAF, and ISAF and the SCR are not required to speak to counterparts in Afghanistan with a single NATO voice.[53]

U.S. Forces in Afghanistan

The U.S. footprint in Afghanistan, and command and control arrangements for U.S. forces deployed there, have evolved over time, partly in response to the expansion of ISAF's area of responsibility to include all of Afghanistan.

U.S. Command Structure

Since major combat operations in 2001, the U.S. military has maintained a distinct special operations forces (SOF) presence in Afghanistan, reporting to U.S. Special Operations Command (SOCOM). By early 2002, some U.S. conventional forces, including a two-star U.S. Army Division Headquarters, had flowed into Afghanistan, but the footprint remained light—only one brigade combat team (BCT)—until early 2007.

In October 2003, the U.S.-led three-star Combined Forces Command-Afghanistan (CFC-A) was established in Kabul. CFC-A oversaw two U.S.-led two-star commands that also included coalition partners—a training command for the ANSF, and a Combined Joint Task Force (CJTF) of conventional forces in eastern Afghanistan. CFC-A served until ISAF assumed security responsibility for all of Afghanistan, and was then deactivated, in February 2007. Following the deactivation of CFC-A, its subordinate ANSF training command, the Combined Security Transition Command-Afghanistan (CSTC-A), began reporting directly to U.S. Central Command (CENTCOM), and its subordinate CJTF assumed a dual U.S./NATO reporting chain, to CENTCOM for U.S. issues and to ISAF in its NATO capacity as RC-East. In October 2008, the Department of Defense activated United States Forces-Afghanistan (USFOR-A), a new four-star headquarters designed to streamline command and control for U.S. forces operating in Afghanistan. The ISAF Commanding General was given the additional assignment of serving as the USFOR-A Commanding General. As the head of ISAF, General McChrystal reports up the NATO chain of command to SACEUR Admiral James Stavridis; as the head of USFOR-A, he reports to the Commanding General of CENTCOM, General David Petraeus.

U.S. Force Levels

There are currently approximately 72,000 U.S. military personnel in Afghanistan serving ISAF and Operation Enduring Freedom, including Brigade Combat Teams from the following units: 2nd Infantry Division, 10th Mountain Division, 25th Mechanized Infantry Division, 38th Infantry

---

[52] Ambassador Fernando Gentilini, Interview, Kabul, Afghanistan, November 2008.

[53] ISAF officials, Interviews, Kabul, Afghanistan, November 2008.

Division (National Guard), 82nd Airborne Division, 2nd Marine Expeditionary Brigade, and elements of the 7th U.S. Army Special Forces Group. Units identified as scheduled for deployment the spring and summer of 2010 include Brigade Combat Teams from the 34th Infantry Division (National Guard), the 101st Airborne Division, and the 2nd Stryker Cavalry Regiment, the 10th Mountain Division, and the U.S. Marine Regimental Combat Team 2.[54]

Tracking the evolution of U.S. troop commitments to Afghanistan operations, the December 2008 numbers marked a significant increase from two years earlier, in December 2006, when U.S. forces in Afghanistan included only one BCT. In early 2007, an additional BCT was added, by extending the tour of the 3rd BCT, 10th Mountain Division (3/10) by 120 days, flowing in its original replacement, 4th BCT, 82nd Airborne Division, on schedule, and later replacing 3/10 with the 173rd Airborne BCT.[55] In January 2008, the Department of Defense announced that President Bush had approved an "extraordinary, one-time" deployment of 3,200 additional Marines to Afghanistan.[56] Those forces included the 24th Marine Expeditionary Unit (MEU), which served as a combat force in southern Afghanistan, and the 2nd Battalion, 7th Marine Regiment (2/7) who served as advisors for the ANSF. Both units redeployed in November 2008, but a Marine Air Ground Task Force (MAGTF), including 3rd Battalion, 8th Marine Regiment, plus additional logistics and air support, deployed to southern Afghanistan in November 2008 to serve both as battlespace owners—responsible for security in a given area of operations—and as ANSF advisors.

For RC-South, General McKiernan requested a U.S. force package similar to the one in RC-East—that is, three BCTs (or equivalents), an aviation brigade, and key enablers including engineers. He argued that in southern Afghanistan, sufficient international and Afghan security forces are simply not available to "provide for adequate security for the people."[57] U.S. military officials in Afghanistan noted that some areas of southern Afghanistan contain known security challenges that still needed to be addressed—these included Kandahar city, and a part of Garmsir District in Helmand province known as the "fish hook" and long used by insurgents as a base of operations. Other areas, including Nimroz province, were "unknowns" given the lack of international and Afghan forces deployed there. Further areas simply had too few forces to fully clear and hold them—for example, when ISAF assumed responsibility for southern Afghanistan, Romanian forces replaced U.S. forces in Zabul province, but the Romanians had been prepared to conduct stability, not counterinsurgency, operations.[58]

The Obama Administration bolstered U.S. forces levels in the spring of 2009 by an additional 21,000 troops, including 3,000 specifically dedicated to the training of Afghan National Security Forces. The additional combat forces, according to U.S. commanders in Afghanistan, flowed primarily into Kandahar, Helmand, and Zabul provinces.[59]

---

[54] DOD press release, "DOD Announces Units for Afghanistan Rotations and Deployments," December 22, 2009.

[55] See Matthew Cox, "10th Mountain Brigade Extended in Afghanistan," *Army Times,* January 25, 2007.

[56] See Ann Scott Tyson, "3,200 Marines to Deploy to Afghanistan in Spring," *Washington Post,* January 16, 2008.

[57] General David McKiernan, Atlantic Council, Washington, DC, November 18, 2008, transcript available at http://www.acus.org/event_blog/general-david-d-mckiernan-speaks-councils-commanders-series/transcript.

[58] Interviews with ISAF officials, Kabul and Kandahar, Afghanistan, November 2008.

[59] ISAF officials, Interviews, Kabul and Kandahar, November 2008.

Key Enablers

U.S. commanders and officials in Afghanistan stress the need for sufficient enablers to support the growing force. Engineers are critical, they underscore, to support both the construction of any additional defense infrastructure required by the deployment of additional forces, and to play a supporting role in reconstruction efforts.

Aviation is critical for both combat operations and also—especially—for air mobility in a country whose lack of infrastructure and forbidding terrain severely limit the utility of ground transportation. Ground vehicles, in turn, must be well-suited for their proposed use on Afghanistan's rugged terrain. Some U.S. troops have reportedly found that Mine-Resistant Ambush-Protected (MRAP) armored fighting vehicles, which have provided life-saving protection against improvised explosive devices (IEDs) in Iraq, are less well-suited to Afghanistan's unpaved roads and off-road requirements.[60]

Current Intelligence, Surveillance and Reconnaissance (ISR) assets are, according to one U.S. commander, "not even in the ballpark," and, according to a senior ISAF official, ground units "are screaming for more assets."[61] A former U.S. battalion commander in Afghanistan argued after his tour, "As a rule, each battalion-sized task force should have constant unmanned aerial vehicle and close-air-support coverage."[62] In 2008, Secretary Gates, recognizing a need to provide troops in the field with improved ISR assets, formed an ISR task force to assess requirements and speed the process of meeting warfighter needs.[63] A CENTCOM ISR Task Force is in the process of providing additional personnel and assets for U.S. forces in Afghanistan.

Language capability is also essential, in order to support the ability of U.S. forces to follow the key counterinsurgency injunction to live with the population, and requirements will grow proportionally with increases in U.S. ground forces in Afghanistan. The need is complicated by the fact that Afghanistan's two official languages—Dari and Pashto—are not mutually intelligible, and many Afghans know one but not the other. One option is to utilize U.S. servicemembers with local language ability, but such troops may be in short supply. Dari and Pashto are regarded as difficult languages to learn, requiring time to develop the ability to communicate in either of them on substantive matters. Another option is to utilize Afghan interpreters. One challenge is that, in addition to the general challenge of sufficient supply, Afghan languages vary from region to region; in some situations, a non-local Afghan interpreter might be understood but nevertheless regarded with some suspicion as an outsider. Variations in regional dialect English-language instruction now available to members of the Afghan National Security Forces might also ease some mil-to-mil communication barriers, but will not directly help U.S. forces communicate with local populations.

---

[60] See Nancy A. Youssef, "U.S. Marines Find Iraq Tactics Don't Work in Afghanistan," McClatchy Newspapers, January 11, 2009. For background on MRAPs, see CRS Report RS22707, *Mine-Resistant, Ambush-Protected (MRAP) Vehicles: Background and Issues for Congress*, by Andrew Feickert.

[61] TF Currahee and ISAF officials, Interviews, Khowst province and Kabul, Afghanistan, November 2008. Under General McKiernan's predecessor, ISAF went from two to four Predator lines.

[62] Christopher D. Kolenda, "How to Win in Afghanistan," *Weekly Standard*, October 13, 2008.

[63] See Secretary of Defense Robert Gates, Remarks, Air War College, Maxwell Air Force Base, Alabama, April 21, 2008, available at http://www.defenselink.mil/speeches/speech.aspx?speechid=1231. Secretary Gates said: "My concern is that our services are still not moving aggressively in wartime to provide resources needed now on the battlefield. I've been wrestling for months to get more intelligence, surveillance, and reconnaissance assets into the theatre. ...While we've doubled this capability in recent months, it is still not good enough."

Legal Basis for Presence of International Forces

Two separate sets of arrangements are in place, for ISAF and for U.S. forces deployed under U.S. command, to provide a legal basis for the presence of those forces in Afghanistan.

Legal Basis for U.S. Forces

In 2002 and 2003, U.S. Embassy Kabul and the Afghan Ministry for Foreign Affairs exchanged diplomatic notes, which together constituted a formal agreement. The notes, which remain in force, confirmed that military and civilian personnel of the Department of Defense shall be accorded a status equivalent to that of Embassy administrative and technical staff under the 1961 Vienna Convention on Diplomatic Relations. The notes also addressed freedom of movement, licenses, the wearing of uniforms, the use of vehicles, exemption from taxation, and imports and exports. They confirmed U.S. criminal jurisdiction over U.S. personnel.[64]

Some of the basic provisions of that exchange of notes were reconfirmed by a joint declaration signed by President Karzai and President Bush, in May 2005, in which the two countries committed themselves to a strategic partnership with the goal of "strengthen[ing] U.S.-Afghan ties to help ensure Afghanistan's long-term security, democracy and prosperity." The Declaration confirmed the bilateral intent to work together closely on a range of activities including, in the security sector: ANSF training, security sector reform, counterterrorism operations, counternarcotics programs, intelligence-sharing, border security, and strengthening ties with NATO. The Declaration included the specific, practical commitment that U.S. military forces operating in Afghanistan would continue to have access to Bagram Air Base "and facilities at other locations as may be mutually determined," and that U.S. and coalition forces would continue to enjoy freedom of action to conduct military operations "based on consultations and pre-agreed procedures."[65]

Legal Basis for ISAF Forces

United Nations Security Council Resolutions (UNSCR) provide the legal basis for the presence of ISAF forces in Afghanistan. A December 2001 UNSCR authorized, under Chapter VII of the United Nations Charter, the establishment of ISAF to "assist...in the maintenance of security in Kabul and its surrounding areas."[66] That mandate was based on a specific appeal for such a force included in the December 2001 Bonn Agreement.[67] In January 2002, the Interim Authority of Afghanistan signed a Military Technical Agreement with the newly formed ISAF.

---

[64] See "Diplomatic Note No.202," Embassy of the United States of America, Kabul, Afghanistan, September 26, 2002; "Note, Document No.791," Transitional Islamic State of Afghanistan, Ministry of Foreign Affairs, Fifth Political Department, December 12, 2002; and "Note, Document No.93," Transitional Islamic State of Afghanistan, Ministry of Foreign Affairs, American and Canada Political Affairs Department, May 28, 2003. See also Karen DeYoung, "Only a Two-Page 'Note' Governs U.S. Military in Afghanistan," *Washington Post*, August 28, 2008.

[65] See Joint Declaration of the United States-Afghanistan Strategic Partnership, May 23, 2005, available at available at http://www.whitehouse.gov/news/releases/2005/05/20050523-2.html.

[66] S/RES/1386 (2001), December 20, 2001.

[67] See Annex I, "International Security Force," *Agreement on Provisional Arrangements in Afghanistan Pending the Re-Establishment of Permanent Government Institutions*, Bonn, Germany, December 5, 2001, available at http://www.mfa.gov.af/Documents/ImportantDoc/The%20Bonn%20Agreement.pdf. The Agreement states: "This force will assist in the maintenance of security for Kabul and its surrounding areas. Such a force could, as appropriate, be (continued...)

In October 2003, the UN Security Council authorized an expansion of the ISAF mandate to include supporting GIRoA in maintaining security outside Kabul and its environs, and providing security to support the accomplishment of other objectives outlined in the Bonn Agreement.[68] The current UN mandate extends the authorization of ISAF for a period of 12 months beyond October 13, 2009.[69]

GIRoA Concerns

Over time, the Afghan leadership has expressed interest in making sure that ISAF- and U.S.-led forces coordinate their operations with the ANSF and with each other. For example, the 2006 Afghanistan Compact, the basic framework for international community engagement in Afghanistan in all sectors, states that all "OEF counter-terrorism operations will be conducted in close coordination with the Afghan Government and ISAF."[70]

In August 2008, President Karzai called for a review of the presence of all foreign forces in Afghanistan and the conclusion of formal status of forces agreements.[71] He issued the call during the heated U.S.-Iraqi negotiation process aimed at achieving a status of forces-like agreement, and just after U.S. airstrikes in Azizabad, Afghanistan, had apparently produced a number of civilian casualties. In January 2009, GIRoA reportedly sent a proposed draft agreement to NATO, which outlined terms and conditions for the presence of NATO forces in Afghanistan.[72]

Security Situation

The year 2009 witnessed an increase in security incidents that led some observers to argue that the insurgency was gaining ground—that the Taliban was "winning"—while others argued instead that insurgent tactics were evolving. The insurgency remained a loose and sometimes internally fractious network of Afghans, supported by some outside help including the availability of safe haven across the border in Pakistan.

Security Trends: Characterization

In general, the security climate in Afghanistan has tended to follow cyclical patterns, based on the seasons. The spring poppy harvest season draws some workers-for-hire away from the insurgency; insurgent leaders, who profit from the poppy crop, support this pattern. The forbidding winter cold makes movement and many activities harder, and usually finds some insurgents recuperating across the border in Pakistan. The warmer spring weather provides an

---

(...continued)

progressively expanded to other urban centers and areas."

[68] S/RES/1510 (2003), October 13, 2003.

[69] UNSCR 1890 (2009), October 8, 2009.

[70] *The Afghanistan Compact: Building on Success*, London Conference on Afghanistan, London, UK, February 1, 2006, available at http://www.nato.int/isaf/docu/epub/pdf/afghanistan_compact.pdf.

[71] See Karen DeYoung, "Only a Two-Page 'Note' Governs U.S. Military in Afghanistan," *Washington Post*, August 28, 2008.

[72] See Associated Press, "Afghanistan Seeks More Control of NATO Troops," *Los Angeles Times*, January 21, 2009.

opportunity for insurgents to attempt operations. Given the cyclical patterns, changes in security trends are best evaluated by year-to-year rather than month-to-month comparisons.

Recent years, by all accounts, have witnessed an upswing in security incidents. Many practitioners date the growing violence from mid-2006, when NATO assumed security responsibility first for southern, and then for eastern Afghanistan. Minister of Defense Wardak, for example, noted that in 2006 the insurgents "came on in a big way," and suggested that their intent had been to weaken political will in NATO capitals.[73]

ISAF officials note that from 2007 to 2008, there was a 33% increase in the overall number of kinetic events. ISAF defines "kinetic" events to include attacks against Afghan or international forces, whether by improvised explosive device (IED), indirect fire, or direct fire; but not, for example, kidnappings or intimidation. IED events, the single largest cause of casualties, increased by 27%. In addition, attacks on GIRoA officials and facilities increased by 119%. Afghan civilian deaths, in turn, increased by between 40 and 46%.[74]

The FY2008 National Defense Authorization Act requires the Department of Defense to provide a semi-annual report to Congress describing the state of security and stability in Afghanistan. The latest report, released in June 2009, was prepared in coordination with the Department of State, the Director of National Intelligence, the Department of Justice, the Drug Enforcement Administration, the Agency for International Development, and the Department of Agriculture. Among the report's observations are the following items:

- Insurgent attacks increased 60% over the same reporting period in 2008.

- Though military casualties, both international and Afghan increased 48%, civilian casualties decreased 9%.

- Insurgent activities were more widespread and at a higher intensity.

- Although NATO allies increased their contributions, NATO's Combined Joint Statement of Requirements for ISAF remained unfulfilled in terms both personnel and equipment.

- Many contributing nations continue to maintain "caveats" or restrictions on how their troops be of use, often prohibiting offensive combat, and thereby constraining their forces' usefulness.

Security Trends: Evaluation

These developments led some observers to conclude that the balance had tipped in favor of the insurgency. A study by the Paris-based International Council on Security and Development, released in December 2008, concluded that "…the Taliban has been experiencing a renaissance that has gained momentum since 2005. The West is in genuine danger of losing Afghanistan."[75] In

---

[73] Minister of Defense of Afghanistan Abdul Rahim Wardak, Interview, Kabul, Afghanistan, November 2008.

[74] "Metrics Brief 2007-2008," International Security Assistance Force, January 2009. The range for Afghan civilian deaths reflects differences between ISAF and UNAMA data collection. UNAMA figures reflect a lower percentage increase, but higher absolute numbers of deaths. ISAF explains that UNAMA's capacity to investigate and verify reports, *inter alia* to prevent duplication, is more limited than ISAF's, ISAF official, personal communication, January 2009.

[75] See Yochi Dreazen, "Taliban Expanding Foothold in Afghanistan, Report Finds," *Wall Street Journal,* December 8, (continued...)

---

a December 2008 Op-Ed, former head of UNAMA Lakhdar Brahimi wrote: "The [Afghan] government is losing ground every day to insurgents and other outlaws who now control at least a third of the country."[76] After embedding with Taliban fighters, journalist Nir Rosen concluded that the Taliban was winning.[77]

ISAF officials explain the increased number of security incidents somewhat differently. They point out that the growing presence of "friendly" forces, including international troops and Afghan forces—including 11 new Afghan National Army battalions and 10,000 more ISAF troops, from November 2007 to November 2008—allowed the conduct of more operations, and thus more contact with the enemy. They add that deteriorating control of the border areas of Pakistan provided insurgents with additional safe haven opportunities.[78]

ISAF commanders also stress the importance of evaluating insurgent attacks qualitatively, as well as quantitatively. By late summer 2008, under pressure from international and ANSF operations, insurgents abandoned large-scale, relatively conventional-style attacks, because they were suffering heavy losses. Insurgent groups moved instead toward small-unit operations, applying more asymmetrical and more sophisticated tactics. These included attacks on key lines of communication (LOCs) including roads and bridges, more use of IEDs, assassination attempts against Afghan civilian and military officials, and attacks against government facilities such as district centers and schools. Insurgents, officials suggest, are "getting more effective" at these asymmetric activities. The specific impact of insurgent targeting of LOCs is hard to measure, ISAF officials note, since no systematic measure is made of highway traffic.[79]

At the same time, ISAF officials assess that the Taliban and other insurgents, while gaining some greater tactical facility, are not guided by a single, coherent strategy—the leadership does not appear to be formulating and directing an overall master plan.[80]

At the end of 2008, senior officials in Afghanistan tended to hedge their bets when describing the security climate. UN SRSG Kai Eide noted: "We haven't lost…but we haven't won…"[81] A senior

---

(...continued)

2008.

[76] Lakhdar Brahimi, "A New Path for Afghanistan," *Washington Post,* December 7, 2008.

[77] Nir Rosen, "How We Lost the War We Won," *Rolling Stone*, October 30, 2008. Rosen appeared to reach the conclusion that the Taliban was winning in part because they told him so; for example, one of his hosts noted, "From now on, it's all Taliban territory – the Americans and police don't come here at night." Of course, the same methodological questions, concerning reliance on the statements of one's informants, could also be applied to field interviews with "friendly" forces. Rosen's article also prompted some debate concerning the ethics of embedding with insurgent forces. See also Paul Watson, "Behind the Lines with the Taliban," *Los Angeles Times,* January 11, 2009. Watson, who briefly embedded with Taliban fighters in Ghazni province south of Kabul, concluded that the area was "Taliban country" where the Taliban were in charge. He quotes one fighter as saying, "Police and soldiers can never come to our territory. If they do, they won't go back safe and sound."

[78] General David McKiernan and other ISAF officials, Interviews, Kabul, Afghanistan, November 2008.

[79] See General David McKiernan, Atlantic Council, Washington, DC, November 18, 2008, transcript available at http://www.acus.org/event_blog/general-david-d-mckiernan-speaks-councils-commanders-series/transcript; and MG Robert Cone, DOD Press Briefing, November 12, 2008, available at http://www.defenselink.mil/transcripts/transcript.aspx?transcriptid=4314. Also, U.S. commanders, Interviews, November 2008.

[80] ISAF officials, Interviews, Kabul, Afghanistan, November 2008. General McKiernan added that overall, the Taliban is "less than the sum of its parts."

[81] UN SRSG Kai Eide, Interview, Kabul, Afghanistan, November 2008.

U.S. military official described it this way: "We're winning the fight, but not the war."[82] Some COIN theorists argue, in turn, that such uncertainty is not neutral—that in a COIN fight, "not winning" is tantamount to losing.

Characterizing the Insurgency[83]

While many observers use the term "Taliban" as a short-hand for the insurgency in Afghanistan, senior western officials in Afghanistan stress that the insurgency is not unified. ISAF prefers the term "insurgent syndicate" to refer collectively to all its various strands. Further, insurgent activities are closely linked with criminality, always a potent force in ungoverned spaces, and in particular with drug cultivation and sales.

Taliban

The Taliban itself, Afghan and ISAF officials note, is more a network than a single organization.[84] The Taliban emerged from the Afghan civil war of the early and mid-1990's, and the organization ruled Afghanistan from its capture of Kabul in 1996 until its defeat in 2001. Mullah Mohammed Omar, the *de facto* head of state during Taliban rule, is generally assumed to be alive and leading the organization from Pakistan. In December 2008, for example, he reportedly issued new threats over the Internet against international forces in Afghanistan.[85] The Taliban leadership includes two main "shuras" (councils)—a leadership council in Quetta, Pakistan, under Mullah Omar's watch, and another shura based in Peshawar, Pakistan.[86] The Taliban reportedly receives support from some current and/or former Pakistani officials, including members of the Inter-Services Intelligence Directorate (ISI), in the form of logistics, medical, and training assistance.[87]

Haqqani Network

The Haqqani network is closely associated with the Taliban and one of its strongest factions. Reportedly, the network is also particularly closely linked to al Qaeda. Jalaluddin Haqqani fought as a mujahedin leader against Soviet forces, receiving substantial assistance from the CIA by way of Pakistan's ISI.[88] When the Taliban came to power, he joined the government as a Minister but retained a separate power base in his home Zadran district and tribe, east of Kabul. His son Sirajudin has reportedly ascended to a key leadership role, and has reportedly called for changes in the leadership of the Quetta shura. U.S. officials in Afghanistan note that Sirajudin, like his

---

[82] U.S. military official, Interview, Kabul, Afghanistan, November 2008.

[83] For background about insurgent groups in Afghanistan, see Seth G. Jones, *Counterinsurgency in Afghanistan*, (Santa Monica, CA: RAND Corporation, 2008).

[84] On the Taliban in general, see Major Shahid Afsar, Pakistan Army, Major Chris Samples, U.S. Army, and Major Thomas Wood, U.S. Army, "The Taliban: An Organizational Analysis," *Military Review,* vo. 88, no. 3 (May-June 2008).

[85] Reuters, "Taliban's Murderous Mullah Threatens West," *New York Post*, December 8, 2008.

[86] See Mohammad Masoom Stanekzai, "Thwarting Afghanistan's Insurgency: A Pragmatic Approach toward Peace and Reconciliation," United States Institute of Peace, September 2008. Stanekzai, who held a fellowship at the U.S. Institute of Peace, was previously a senior GIRoA official.

[87] See Seth G. Jones, *Counterinsurgency in Afghanistan,* (Santa Monica, CA: RAND Corporation, 2008).

[88] For background about Haqqani, see Jay Solomon, "Troubled Border: Failed Courtship of Warlord Trips up U.S. in Afghanistan," *The Wall Street Journal,* November 8, 2007.

father, has focused on his home Zadran district but has also expanded his activities into the areas south of Kabul.

Hezb-i-Islami Gulbuddin (HiG)

Gulbuddin Hekmatyar was a key mujahedin leader against Soviet forces. His organization, then known as the Hezb-e-Islami, received substantial aid from the U.S. government, which reportedly considered him a key ally. He twice held the title of Prime Minister during the early 1990's civil war period, before seeking refuge in Iran when the Taliban came to power. He has re-emerged in Afghanistan as the leader of the insurgent group, Hezb-i-Islami Gulbuddin (HiG), which is affiliated with both the Taliban and al Qaeda. In 2008, Hekmatyar apparently opened the door to talks with GIRoA, in part through a spring 2008 letter addressed to President Karzai. Some practitioners and observers suggest that there may be good potential for drawing Hekmatyar away from the insurgent fight and into a constructive role.[89] Others caution that his reputation for Islamic extremism and human rights abuses call into question the likelihood and advisability of any reconciliation with him.

Foreign Groups

Foreign groups play critical roles in the insurgency by variously supporting and enabling Afghan insurgents.[90]

Al Qaeda, which both enabled and leveraged the Taliban during its years in power, reportedly mobilizes foreign fighters from the Arab world, Chechnya, Uzbekistan, and other locations, to join the fight in Afghanistan.

Tehrik Taliban-i Pakistan (TTiP) is an umbrella organization for indigenous Pakistani Taliban commanders, based in Pakistan, in the Federally Administered Tribal Areas (FATA) along the border with Afghanistan. TTiP is led by Baitullah Mahsud, who is from South Waziristan in the FATA, and who has reportedly built up strongholds in North and South Waziristan by recruiting and training young men, and "killing uncooperative tribal leaders."[91]

Lashkar-e-Tayba, a Pakistani insurgent group originally focused on the disputed Kashmir region, reportedly cuts its insurgent teeth along the border with Afghanistan by training insurgents to fight there.

Tehrik Nefaz-e Shariat Mohammadi (TNSM) is a Pakistani insurgent group based primarily in the Northwest Frontier Province next to the FATA. Focused primarily on deepening its local control, the TNSM has also supported some Taliban operations in Afghanistan.[92]

---

[89] ISAF senior officials, Interviews, Kabul, Afghanistan, November 2008. See Anna Mulrine, "Afghan Warlords, Formerly Backed by the CIA, Now Turn their Guns on U.S. Troops," *U.S. News and World Report,* July 11, 2008.

[90] For a concise discussion of Afghan insurgent groups and foreign groups supporting the insurgency, see Mohammad Masoom Stanekzai, "Thwarting Afghanistan's Insurgency: A Pragmatic Approach toward Peace and Reconciliation," United States Institute of Peace, September 2008.

[91] See Jane Perlez, "Taliban Leader Flaunts Power Inside Pakistan," *The New York Times,* June 2, 2008; "Tribal tribulations: The Pakistani Taliban in Waziristan," *Jane's Intelligence Review,* January 13, 2009; and "Tehrik-e-Taliban Pakistan," *Jane's Terrorism and Insurgency Centre,* January 13, 2009.

[92] See Rahimullah Yusufzai, "The emergence of the Pakistani Taliban," *Jane's Terrorism and Insurgency Centre,* (continued...)

Popular Support for the Insurgency?

The population is the center of gravity—the primary focus—in counterinsurgency operations. Evaluating a population's support, tacit as well as active, for an insurgency, as well as its perceptions of the fight, is one helpful tool for assessing the strength of that insurgency.

In general, it is common for insurgents to try to shape popular perceptions. Some experts argue that in 2008 in Afghanistan, the Taliban and other insurgents used high-profile attacks in and near Kabul to sow fear, or create a "sense of siege."[93] Those attacks included, among others, a strike against the opulent and popular Serena Hotel in January, an assassination attempt against President Karzai in April, a bombing at the Indian Embassy in July, and the kidnapping of International Rescue Committee workers in August.

Meanwhile, in late 2009, ISAF officials assessed that active Afghan popular support for the Taliban and other insurgents was not increasing—not least because the Taliban's ideology had little appeal for most Afghans. At the same time, ISAF assessed that popular support was shifting away from the government of Afghanistan toward "fence-sitting," driven by frustrations with poor governance, lack of economic progress, corruption, and lack of security. COIN theory underscores the importance of at least tacit popular support for the government—that popular neutrality is insufficient to defeat an insurgency.

COIN Operations

At least as important to the success of the counterinsurgency as the number of Afghan and international security forces, experts argue, is what those forces actually do. As a rule, counter-insurgencies share an emphasis on "population security," but circumstances, and therefore the most effective approaches, may vary widely from one COIN campaign to another, or even geographically or temporally within a given COIN campaign.[94] In Afghanistan, COIN efforts have been challenged by especially rugged terrain, by limited forces and resources, and by the need to gain sufficient understanding of local areas to develop situation-specific approaches.

Shape, Clear, Hold, Build

In Afghanistan, COIN terminology, if not yet practice, has become a lingua franca shared by Afghan and international practitioners. The basic tenet of COIN operations in Afghanistan, borrowed and adapted from Vietnam and more recently Iraq, is "shape, clear, hold, build." In general, that approach includes working closely with Afghan counterparts to target insurgents, kinetically if so required; using Afghan or if necessary international security forces to hold an

---

(...continued)

December 11, 2007.

[93] James Kitfield, "Progress in Afghanistan gets rockier," *National Journal,* September 15, 2008. See also Sami Yousafzai and Ron Moreau, "The Taliban's Baghdad Strategy," *Newsweek,* August 4, 2008. The article cites a "senior Taliban intelligence operative in Pakistan" as stating that by focusing on Kabul "we can create panic and undermine the last vestiges of support for the regime."

[94] General David Petraeus, U.S. CENTCOM Commanding General, recently stated, "Every case is unique. ...While general concepts that proved important in Iraq may be applicable to Afghanistan....the application of those 'big ideas ' has to be adapted to Afghanistan." General David Petraeus, Interview, *Foreign Policy,* (January/ February 2009), available at http://www.foreignpolicy.com/story/cms.php?story_id=4587.

---

area once it is cleared; and applying coordinated civil-military efforts to begin building institutions and services once the security landscape in an area so permits.

COIN efforts in Konar province in eastern Afghanistan, along the border with Pakistan, are frequently presented as an instructive model of coordinated civil-military action. There, a U.S. Army battalion working with a very capable Afghan National Army (ANA) unit first cleared the area, and then established outposts to provide presence. U.S. forces, supported by a Provincial Reconstruction Team, then negotiated deals with local tribal shuras—if the shuras would provide security, they would receive economic development "in the form of roads, bridges, schools and health clinics." Central to the approach was the construction of a paved road—a rarity outside big cities in Afghanistan—in which local residents had a vested interest. The road gave forces the access they needed to secure village populations, it made it harder for insurgents to emplace IEDs, it gave civilian assistance agencies freedom of movement, and it gave local residents a critical tool to support economic development. The U.S. Commanders Emergency Response Program (CERP) funded payments to locals to provide security for the road.[95]

Practitioners stress, however, that there is no cookie-cutter model for COIN in Afghanistan—roads, for example, cannot always play the role they did in Konar province. In 2009, insurgents stepped up their attacks against Afghanistan's major road arteries, include Highway 1 that connects Kabul with Kandahar. Officials speculated that the insurgents attacking the highway in Zabul wanted to tie up the ANA and other forces, forcing them to build check points and leaving them fewer resources to focus on insurgent strongholds. In southern Zabul province, along the Highway 1 artery, military and civilian officials wondered if the "Konar model" approach to roads might be applicable. What they discovered, however, is that roads served a different function in Zabul—the highway was used primarily by inter-state truck drivers and the insurgents themselves, while local residents required only some passable means for getting to and from local markets. In other words, local residents did not perceive that they had the same, strong vested interest in the security of the main highway as residents of Konar province had in their own road.

Operations by the U.S. Marines, in the town of Garmsir in southern Helmand Province also reflected some key COIN approaches including an emphasis on population security, close cooperation with local security forces, the use of both kinetic and soft tools, and the incorporation of civilian resources. By the time operations commenced, Garmsir had become a key insurgent transit and logistics hub, and much of the local population had withdrawn. The action began with a large-scale aerial insertion, followed by a month of clearing and fighting against small but tenacious and well dug-in insurgent groups. As the insurgents were defeated in a given area, the local population began to return, and the Marines increased their focus on population security, including the use of "gated communities" for population control, and reaching out to community leaders. As the fighting wound down, the ANSF joined the Marines on patrols to provide presence and "hold" the area. From the planning stages onward, the Marines worked with the U.S. Agency for International Development, asking, "What do we want this to look like, afterwards?" The AID representative working with the 24th MEU was ready to initiate projects as soon as the security situation so allowed.[96]

---

[95] See David Kilcullen, "Road-Building in Afghanistan: Part 1 of a Series on Political Maneuver in Counterinsurgency," *Small Wars Journal,* April 24, 2008, available at http://smallwarsjournal.com/blog/2008/04/political-maneuver-in-counteri/; and David Ignatius, "Building Bridges in the Back of Beyond," *Washington Post,* May 1, 2008.

[96] 24th MEU officials, Interviews, Kandahar, Afghanistan, November 2008.

ISAF commanders stress that through 2009, insufficient international and Afghan forces were available to shape, clear, hold, and build effectively throughout Afghanistan. The ISAF 2009 winter campaign, for example, conducted in selected districts chosen to include the majority of the Afghan population, aimed to "hold" ground and deepen security there, without significantly expanding GIRoA's control geographically.

Living Among the Population

As a rule, the center of any counterinsurgency is the population, and living among the population is a central tenet of COIN. As CENTCOM Commanding General, General David Petraeus, and many others have stressed, "You don't commute to work."[97] Senior officials at U.S.-led RC-East noted that as of late 2008, RC-East had between 130 and 140 combat outposts (COPs) in their area of responsibility (AOR)—"We're really out with the people." Most of those COPs were co-located with ANA counterparts or supported nearby Afghan observation posts, although a few were U.S.-only.[98]

For some Allies, constrained by national caveats, the premise of living among the population is a challenge. The idea is generally understood to mean getting outside the wire and interacting with the population as much as possible, not merely living adjacent to it. Allied forces that are largely confined to forward operating bases (FOBs) cannot follow the approach.

For ISAF in general, a major constraint on living with the population has been insufficient international forces. As one commander argued, "The strategy doesn't work when you don't have enough forces to do it."[99] Writing about U.S. efforts in both Afghanistan and Iraq, leading defense expert Colonel H.R. McMaster noted: "Decisions against deploying coalition forces in numbers sufficient to secure populations left many commanders with no other option than to adopt a raiding approach to counterinsurgency operations—an approach that tended to reinforce the perception of coalition forces as aggressors and conflated tactical successes with actual measures of strategic effectiveness."[100]

It might seem that by scaling back the size of the force presence at each outpost, the number of outposts could be increased and the overall footprint of forces "living with the population" could be extended. The problem is that, according to commanders on the ground, it takes one platoon to secure an outpost, so getting forces outside the wire to interact with the population requires two platoons at each location. RC-East noted that about 40 of its COPs were single platoon-sized, with 30 Soldiers or fewer.

Afghanistan itself presents some particular challenges to living among the population—the Afghan population is much more rural and dispersed than that of Iraq, and many Afghans live in remote, isolated, and barely accessible valleys. Determining how best to live among the population may also sometimes require some discretion. Some practitioners and experts contend that in many long-isolated valleys, the local population is generally hostile to all outsiders,

---

[97] See for example General David Petraeus, COIN Guidance, Multi-National Force Iraq, 2008.

[98] RC-East officials, Interviews, Bagram, Afghanistan, November 2008.

[99] RC-East official, Interview, Bagram, Afghanistan, November 2008.

[100] H.R. McMaster, "The Human Element: When Gadgetry Becomes Strategy," *World Affairs*, Winter 2009.

whether "friendly" or otherwise. Insisting on living among them create new tensions, without necessarily strengthening that population's resistance to outside insurgents.

Borders

In general, successful counterinsurgency requires a closed system, so that COIN can gradually smother the insurgency. As discussed below, Afghanistan's open border with Pakistan significantly complicates the COIN effort. The border marks the boundary of the system for Afghan and international security forces, constrained by international law, but not for insurgents who make ample use of safe haven and resupply in Pakistan.

Role of Special Operations Forces in COIN

Special operations forces (SOF) play an essential role in COIN in Afghanistan, through direct action against insurgent leaders. One senior U.S. commander underscored SOF's "continuous disruptive effect on leadership." SOF efforts in Afghanistan include significant Allied as well as U.S. participation, as well as a growing role for elite Afghan "commando" forces.

The partnership between U.S. SOF and conventional forces in Afghanistan may differ somewhat from the analogous partnership in Iraq, due to the disparity in the size of the conventional force presence. In Iraq, especially in 2007 and 2008, a large conventional ground forces presence with a widely distributed footprint was able to gain substantial, detailed situational awareness about local conditions, and to provide that insight to SOF for use in targeting, and in planning operations. Further, the much larger conventional presence in Iraq made forces readily available to "hold" a given area once SOF cleared it. The significantly smaller conventional forces presence in Afghanistan may not yet have allowed the development such a robust SOF/conventional synergy.

Role of Air Power in COIN

The major combat phase of operations in Afghanistan relied heavily on ground SOF calling in airstrikes on al Qaeda and Taliban targets, and many experts pointed to those operations as a model of jointness—the ability of Military Services to work together seamlessly. Since then, due to Afghanistan's forbidding, mountainous geography, and to the relative dearth of Afghan and international ground forces, the COIN campaign has continued to rely greatly on the use of kinetic air power. A larger ground forces presence may reduce some of that reliance, but the terrain alone is likely to make air strikes a necessary counterpart to ground-based fires.[101]

Civilian casualties resulting from air strikes in Afghanistan have prompted strong expressions of concern from Afghan and international audiences. President Karzai strongly condemned a coalition air strike conducted on August 22, 2008, against the village of Azizabad, in Herat Province in western Afghanistan, which he said killed 95 Afghan civilians. Further complicating

---

[101] For a recent analysis of the kinetic use of air in Afghanistan, which argues against "excessive restraint in the use of airstrikes," see Lara M. Dadkhah, "Close Air Support and Civilian Casualties in Afghanistan," *Small Wars Journal*, December 30, 2008, available at http://smallwarsjournal.com/blog/2008/12/close-air-support-and-civilian/.

the incident were initial reports from the coalition that apparently conflicted with the numbers claimed by Afghan government officials and local residents.[102]

UNAMA further raised the stakes by issuing an early statement claiming "convincing evidence" that at least 90 civilians, most of them children, had been killed.[103] UN SRSG Kai Eide later asserted that he had been correct to strongly underscore the UN's grave concern with civilian casualties.[104] In a December 2008 interview, Eide warned again of the need to conduct military operations with care, and to guard against civilian casualties, stating, "I am not convinced that we are" listening to the concerns of President Karzai and the Afghan people.[105]

In September 2008, General McKiernan issued an ISAF Tactical Directive, which replaced a directive issued by his predecessor General Dan McNeill in June 2007. This Directive stressed "proportionality, restraint, and utmost discrimination in the use of firepower." It provided specific conditions for the use of air-to-ground munitions, and underscored the need to minimize the risk to civilians.[106] In July 2009, General McChrystal issued a revised Tactical Directive re-emphasizing the need for restraint in using close air support. Though the Directive itself remains classified, ISAF Headquarters released portions of it in unclassified form. Specifically, the Directive states: "The use of air-to-ground munitions and indirect fires against residential compounds is only authorized under very limited and prescribed conditions"[107]

Regional Context

Afghan officials, and international practitioners and observers, generally agree that Afghanistan's security is intimately linked to its relationships with its neighbors, first of all Pakistan, and to relations among those neighbors. General McKiernan stated in late 2008, "This is a regional insurgency and it requires regional solutions."[108] General Petraeus added in early 2009, "In fact, those seeking to help Afghanistan and Pakistan need to widen the aperture even farther, to encompass at least the Central Asian states, India, Iran and even China and Russia."[109] By the end of 2008, most U.S. strategists had concluded that to be successful, a strategy for "Afghanistan" would need to address the broader region. This assessment was reinforced by the Obama Administration's policy review and the subsequent March 2009 White House announcements concerning its new Afghanistan strategy.[110]

A major challenge to the counterinsurgency effort in Afghanistan is the fact that the Afghanistan-Pakistan border is largely porous, and insurgents fighting in Afghanistan have long relied on safe

---

[102] See James Kitfield, "Progress in Afghanistan Gets Rockier," *National Journal,* September 15, 2008; and Carlotta Gall, "Afghan Leader Assails Airstrike He Says Killed 95," *The New York Times,* August 23, 2008.

[103] Candace Rondeaux and Karen DeYoung, "U.N. Finds Airstrike Killed 90 Afghans," *Washington Post*, August 27, 2008.

[104] Kai Eide, Interview, Kabul, Afghanistan, November 2008.

[105] Kirk Semple, "Official Calls for Sensitivity to Afghan Demands," *The New York Times*, December 8, 2008.

[106] ISAF slide, 'Tactical Directive," October 2, 2008.

[107] Memorandum, "Tactical Directive," Headquarters ISAF, July 6, 2009.

[108] General David McKiernan, Interview, Kabul, Afghanistan, November 2008.

[109] General David Petraeus, Interview, Foreign Policy, January/ February 2009, available at http://www.foreignpolicy.com/story/cms.php?story_id=4587.

[110] For a detailed discussion, see CRS Report RL33498, *Pakistan-U.S. Relations*, by K. Alan Kronstadt.

haven and other forms of support in Pakistan. As a rule, counterinsurgency efforts assume a "closed system," in which persistent COIN efforts, and growing popular support, can gradually smother an insurgency, but Pakistan's open border disrupts that premise by giving Afghanistan's insurgents a ready escape hatch.

The insurgency problem is complicated by the fact that the Government of Pakistan (GoP) has traditionally enjoyed only limited control over the Federally Administered Tribal Areas (FATA) that border Afghanistan.[111] The FATA is a legacy of British rule. To boost the border defenses of British India, the British gave semiautonomous status to tribes in that area by creating tribal "agencies," largely responsible for their own security. The area became the "FATA" after independence. Regional experts Barnett Rubin and Ahmed Rashid have argued that today, the area is used as a "staging area" for militants preparing to fight in both Kashmir and in Afghanistan.[112]

Pakistan's turbulent recent history may further complicate the GoP's efforts to achieve control. That history has included the assassination of politician and former Prime Minister Benazir Bhutto in December 2007, just ahead of scheduled general elections. In February 2008, parliamentary elections brought to power a coalition of former opposition parties including Bhutto's Pakistan People's Party, led by her widower Asif Zardari. In August 2008, General Pervez Musharraf, who had come to power in a military coup in 1999, resigned as President of Pakistan. In September 2008, Zardari was elected president, completing a transition to civilian-led rule. The ability and will of that civilian-led government to exercise authority over Pakistan's security forces, and to take steps to stop insurgent activities, is not yet completely clear.

Throughout its short history, Pakistan has had deeply vested interests in Afghanistan. The international border—the British-drawn Durand Line—cuts through territory inhabited, on both sides, by ethnic Pashtuns, with significantly more Pashtuns living in Pakistan than in Afghanistan.[113] The Pashtun population of southern Afghanistan provided the primary base of support for the Taliban during it rise. Further, most observers underscore that the Government of Pakistan has a general interest in ensuring that Afghanistan is a regional ally, in part as a balance against Pakistan's long-simmering conflict with neighboring India. That broad interest was reflected in Pakistani support for the Afghan mujahedin fighting the Soviet occupiers in the 1980's, and later, for the Taliban regime—relationships that have created difficulties in post-Taliban Afghan-Pakistani relations.

In recent years, the GoP attempted to achieve a measure of stability along the border with Afghanistan by following the example of the British Raj and striking a series "truces" with local power brokers, in 2004, 2005, and 2006. In February 2005, for example, the Pakistani military reportedly reached a peace deal with Baitullah Mahsud, leader of the umbrella organization Tehrik Taliban-i Pakistan (TTiP), and withdrew its forces from check points in the region. In mid-

---

[111] For background and analysis of the FATA, see Daniel Markey, "Securing Pakistan's Tribal Belt," Council on Foreign Relations, *Council Special Report* no. 36, August 2008.

[112] See Barnett R. Rubin and Ahmed Rashid, "From Great Game to Grand Bargain: Ending Chaos in Afghanistan and Pakistan," *Foreign Affairs*, vol. 87, no. 6 (November/ December 2008). The authors add, "The area is kept underdeveloped and over-armed as a barrier against invaders."

[113] According to unclassified CIA estimates from July 2008, ethnic Pashtuns comprise 15.42% of Pakistan's population of 172,800,048; and about 42% of Afghanistan's population of 32,738,376. See "Pakistan" and "Afghanistan," The World Fact Book, Central Intelligence Agency, available at https://www.cia.gov/library/publications/the-world-factbook/geos/pk.html and https://www.cia.gov/library/publications/the-world-factbook/geos/af.html.

2006, Islamabad struck a major peace deal with insurgents in North Waziristan, agreeing to end military operations and remove local checkpoints, in return for an end to insurgent attacks on government officials.[114] In early- and mid-2008, Pakistani forces, tried a similar approach, pulling back from TTiP's stronghold in Waziristan in the FATA.[115] By all credible accounts, these "deals" did not lead to greater stability.

In July 2008, the U.S. government reportedly confronted Pakistani authorities with evidence of ties between members of ISI and the Haqqani network in the FATA. At that time, President Bush authorized U.S. military cross-border operations into Pakistan, by ground or Predator unmanned aerial vehicles (UAV). Observers counted at least 11 attacks by Predator UAV in August and September 2008, in addition to a ground attack in early September.[116]

ISAF officials have noted that cross-border attacks have yielded big operational and tactical benefits—by causing the insurgent networks to feel disconnected, and prompting local residents in Pakistan to want al Qaeda and other outsiders to leave their communities.[117] At the same time, U.S. civilian and military officials acknowledge that such cross-border strikes have the potential to spark local protest and to destabilize the fragile Government of Pakistan, still struggling to consolidate civilian rule.

To be clear, NATO's policy for ISAF does not include cross-border strikes. Asked in July 2008 whether the Alliance would go after militants in Pakistan, Secretary-General Jaap de Hoop Scheffer said, "My answer is an unqualified 'no.' We have a United Nations mandate for Afghanistan and that's it. If NATO forces are shot at from the other side of the border, there is always the right to self-defense but you will not see NATO forces crossing into Pakistani territory."[118] The restriction on ISAF forces does not, however, preclude joint operations with the Pakistan to kill or capture individual Taliban leaders.

By late 2008, efforts by the Pakistani military to tackle the insurgency problem had increased noticeably; senior U.S. officials and tactical-level military commanders in Afghanistan attributed the changes to the pressure from U.S. cross-border attacks. In August 2008, the Pakistani military stepped up operations in Bajaur, the northernmost of the seven agencies in the FATA, across from Afghanistan's Konar province. ISAF officials with access to imagery noted that after the operations, Bajaur resembled Fallujah, Iraq, after kinetic coalition operations in November 2004—that is, with some allowances for the more rural setting in Pakistan, destruction from the relatively heavy-handed Bajaur operations was considerable. According to ISAF officials, while the Pakistani operations suggested some room for improvement in the "soft" skills of COIN, they had an impact by disrupting insurgent networks.[119]

---

[114] Text of agreement available at http://www.pbs.org/wgbh/pages/frontline/taliban/etc/nwdeal.html.

[115] See Jane Perlez, "Taliban Leader Flaunts Power Inside Pakistan," *The New York Times*, June 2, 2008, and Jon Hemming, "NATO Beefs Up Forces Along Afghan-Pakistan Border," *Reuters*, May 19, 2008. See also Daniel Markey, "Securing Pakistan's Tribal Belt," Council on Foreign Relations, *Council Special Report* no. 36, August 2008, p. 11.

[116] See Karen DeYoung, "Pakistan Will Give Arms to Tribal Militias," *Washington Post*, October 23, 2008, and Saeed Shah, "Pakistan Rejects 'America's War' on Extremists, *The Guardian*, October 24, 2008.

[117] ISAF, Interviews, Kabul, Afghanistan, November 2008.

[118] Hamid Shalizi, "NATO Chief Says Will Not Hunt Taliban in Pakistan," *Reuters*, July 24, 2008.

[119] U.S. military officials, Interviews, Kabul and Bagram, Afghanistan, November 2008. More than one official cited in this context the phrase from Roman historian Tacitus: "They make a desert and call it peace."

Pakistan's counterinsurgency approaches in the FATA also included arming "lashkars"—militias—of tens of thousands of local residents, to help maintain security.[120] The lashkars, which draw on the strength and local authority of traditional tribal structures, were intended to help "hold" areas after they were cleared by military operations.

2008 also witnessed an improvement in cross-border coordination. Regional Command-East reported that cooperation among Pakistani, Afghan, and U.S. forces continued to grow at the trilateral Border Coordination Center (BCC) at the Torkham Gate, one of six planned BCCs. That collaboration benefited from Predator feeds that provided a common picture of the battlespace. ISAF and their Afghan counterparts planned to establish 6 BCCs by FY2010.[121]

At the tactical level, U.S. ground forces in eastern Afghanistan reported that, the tenor of their regular tactical-level border coordination sessions has grown more constructive. Tactical-level coordination improved—including cases of direct cross-border coordination with Pakistani forces, to "fix and defeat the enemy at the border," particularly along the border with Afghanistan's Paktika province.[122]

Overall, senior U.S. officials in Afghanistan, and outside observers, suggest that substantial improvement of the Afghanistan-Pakistan border situation will require from Pakistan both continued political will and appropriate capabilities. General McKiernan stated in November 2008 that he had seen "a shift in thinking at the senior levels in Pakistan that this insurgency is a problem that threatens the very existence of Pakistan."[123] Other U.S. commanders in Afghanistan noted that they have observed a "sea change" in the views of Pakistani military officials, who increasingly view insurgents as existential threats, and who are attempting to improve the COIN capabilities of Pakistani forces to counter the insurgents. Remaining differences, U.S. military officials suggest, tend to include different perceptions of various insurgent groups and the threats they represent.[124] Other observers suggest that the extent of the commitment of senior Pakistani civilian officials to defeat the insurgent challenge is less clear.

In October 2009, the Pakistani army undertook offensive operations against Taliban strongholds in Waziristan along the eastern border with Afghanistan. Committing upwards of 30,000 troops, these operations continue; however, little information is publically available concerning their progress. Efforts to enlist the support and participation of local tribal leaders in the offensive have been unsuccessful, and the Pakistani desire to keep substantial military forces focused on the Indian border has limited the resources that could be brought to bear in Waziristan. Though U.S. officials have encouraged the Pakistani government to expand these efforts against the Pakistani Taliban, on January 21, 2010, a Pakistani army spokesman indicated that the army was "overstretched" and that no new offensive operations would be mounted in 2010.[125]

---

[120] See Karen DeYoung, "Pakistan Will Give Arms to Tribal Militias," *Washington Post*, October 23, 2008. Such approaches are not new. Just before independence, in 1946, the British government issued a statement noting a reconsideration of its frontier policy. They would now "enlist cooperative tribesmen themselves," rather than simply bombing the area. See "British End Bombing of Indian Tribesmen," *The New York Times,* September 13, 1946.

[121] Major General Jeffrey Schloesser, Interview, Bagram, Afghanistan, November 2008.

[122] Task Force Currahee officials, Interviews, Khowst Province, Afghanistan, November 2008.

[123] General David McKiernan, Atlantic Council, Washington, DC, November 18, 2008, transcript available at http://www.acus.org/event_blog/general-david-d-mckiernan-speaks-councils-commanders-series/transcript.

[124] U.S. military officials, Interviews, Kabul and Bagram, Afghanistan, November 2008.

[125] "Pakistani Army: No New Offensives in 2010", BBC, January 21, 2010.

Observers suggest that a key strategic question concerns the fragility of the Pakistani polity, and the extent to which the GoP can be encouraged or pushed to cooperate in counterinsurgency efforts without significant domestic political blowback. For example, in October 2008, the Pakistani parliament unanimously passed a resolution calling for an end to military action against extremist groups, and its replacement with dialogue. The resolution stressed the need for an "independent foreign policy" for Pakistan, and stated that "the nation stands united against any incursions and invasions of the homeland."[126]

Iran

ISAF officials note that the role of Afghanistan's large neighbor to the west, Iran, is also critical to its future, and they describe Iran's approach as a "dual-track strategy." On one hand, Iran enjoys close, long-standing cultural, linguistic, and religious ties with significant portions of Afghanistan's population. ISAF officials estimate that Iran is the second-largest contributor of reconstruction assistance to Afghanistan, after the United States—its efforts are most evident in Herat Province in western Afghanistan. And since Iran is a major destination for Afghan heroin, with all of its attendant concerns about crime and drug addition, Iranian officials share with their Afghan counterparts a vested interest in effective counternarcotics approaches. Some officials also point to the generally positive role Iran played at the 2001 Bonn Conference, to help forge consensus among Afghan factions about the creation of a post-Taliban government, as evidence that Iran can play a constructive role on Afghan matters.[127]

At the same time, ISAF officials state that Iran has provided some weapons and training to Afghan insurgents. Some add that Tehran may be concerned about a growing U.S. military footprint along both its eastern and western borders, as additional U.S. military forces flow into southern Afghanistan, and U.S. forces assume battlespaces in southern Iraq that were formerly manned by coalition partners. One official argued that Iran's interest is to "keep it simmering" in Afghanistan.[128] Most practitioners and observers suggest that, in some capacity, a comprehensive solution for Afghanistan must take Iran into account.

Afghan National Security Forces (ANSF)[129]

A fundamental premise of counterinsurgency operations is the central importance of host-nation forces—including establishing and improving those forces should their quantity or quality be

---

[126] Saeed Shah, "Pakistan Rejects 'America's War' on Extremists," *The Guardian*, October 24, 2008. This resolution was passed before the late November 2008 terrorist attacks in Mumbai.

[127] On Iran's behavior at the Bonn Conference, see Ambassador James F. Dobbins, *After the Taliban: Nation-Building in Afghanistan*, (Washington, DC: Potomac Books, 2008).

[128] ISAF and U.S. officials, Interviews, Kabul, Bagram, and Kandahar, Afghanistan, November 2008.

[129] *The National Defense Authorization Act for Fiscal Year 2008*, P.L. 110-181, January 28, 2008, §1230, required the Department of Defense to submit a "report on progress toward security and stability in Afghanistan," and §1231 required a report on sustaining the Afghanistan National Security Forces. DOD submitted the first edition of both reports in June 2008. See Department of Defense, *Report on Progress Toward Security and Stability in Afghanistan*, June 2008, available at http://www.defenselink.mil/pubs/ Report_on_Progress_toward_Security_and_Stability_in_Afghanistan_1230.pdf; and Department of Defense, *United States Plan for Sustaining the Afghanistan National Security Forces,* June 2008, available at http://www.defenselink.mil/pubs/ united_states_plan_for_sustaining_the_afghanistan_national_security_forces_1231.pdf.

insufficient. Decades of war, displacement, and mismanagement, followed by the defeat of the Taliban regime, left Afghanistan without organized, functioning security forces or equipment, so rebuilding the Afghan National Security Forces (ANSF) has been a high priority of the post-war international assistance effort. ISAF's broad goal is to transition "lead security responsibility" to the ANSF who are focused, as a rule, on the current fight, not Afghanistan's long-term security requirements. From a security perspective, one positive legacy of the years of conflict may be the fighting spirit so common among many Afghans, acknowledged by the common refrain of international military officials: "They will fight!"

Afghan National Army (ANA)

All of the Afghan security forces are still developing, but the Afghan National Army (ANA), under the Ministry of Defense, is currently, by a wide margin, the most capable force.

ANA Numbers

As of December 2009, approximately 97,000 soldiers were assigned to the ANA. ANA units are participating in 90% of ISAF operations and lead 62% of all joint operations. Of the approximately 90 active battalions (Kandaks), 28 are capable of carrying out operations independently, 30 lead operations with ISAF support, and another 30 participate in operations under ISAF leadership [130]

The Bonn Agreement established an endstrength target of 70,000 for the ANA. A decision was made in early 2008 to stretch that goal to 86,000. In January 2010, the Joint Coordination Monitoring Board (JCMB)—the body co-led by GIRoA and UNAMA, and charged to oversee implementation of the Afghanistan Compact—endorsed GIRoA's plan to increase that target figure to 171,600 by October 2011.

Some outside experts have also strongly advocated programming for a larger ANA. COIN theorist John Nagl, who has helped train U.S. personnel to train the ANSF, argued in November 2008 that the ANA should grow to 250,000.[131] For their part, many Afghan officials share the view that a greater number of troops will be needed.. Minister of Defense Wardak stated that Afghanistan had never yet had the proper proportion of troops to the area to be secured and to the population to be protected. Current force sizing, he noted, assumes the presence of a large international force—which will not always be there, and whose capabilities, he argued, are roughly double that of their Afghan counterparts. He concluded that "between 200,000 and 250,000 would be the proper size for the ANA."[132] In a September 2008 analytical report, a former civilian advisor to President Karzai argued that the ANA endstrength should be "at least 220,000."[133]

---

[130] NATO Factsheet, "Facts and Figures: Afghan National Army," Media Operations Centre, NATO HQ, Brussels, Belgium, December 2009.

[131] "All Things Considered," National Public Radio, November 18, 2008, interview with John Nagl, transcript available at http://www.npr.org/templates/story/story.php?storyId=97170621: ANA should grow to 250,000.

[132] Minister of Defense of Afghanistan Abdul Rahim Wardak, Interview, Kabul, Afghanistan, November 2008.

[133] Mohammad Masoom Stanekzai, "Thwarting Afghanistan's Insurgency: A Pragmatic Approach toward Peace and Reconciliation," United States Institute of Peace, September 2008.

Force Modernization

In 2008, the focus of the ANA itself, and of the coalition ANSF training and advisory effort, was counterinsurgency, with an emphasis on the equipment that could be most readily fielded, and the skills that could most readily be developed and applied to the fight.

One shift, in late 2008, was initial "NATO-ization" of some ANA weapons, first of all a shift from the AK-47 assault rifle of Soviet origins, to the M-16 rifle of U.S. origin, widely used by many NATO countries. The AK-47 was a natural choice, as a starting point—years of Soviet sponsorship and then occupation had made the weapons widely available throughout Afghanistan. In November 2008, the first shipment of M-16's arrived in Kabul, and U.S. trainers began training Afghan army trainers. Some critics have noted that the M-16 is more temperamental to use and maintain than the AK-47, and that it will require an adjustment for Afghan forces. Supporters underscore the operational importance of Afghan interoperability with NATO counterparts.

ANA Corps commanders are focused primarily on the current fight—making sure that their soldiers had the equipment and training necessary for counterinsurgency.[134] Minister of Defense Wardak, however, has taken a longer-term look at possible future requirements, including the traditional military role of providing external defense. That outward-looking perspective was reflected in his suggestion to size the ANA by comparing it with the armies of Afghanistan's neighbors—Pakistan, Iran, and "the bear to the north." To balance between current and future requirements, he urged equipping the ANA "with a mix, right from the beginning, so it works for COIN and later on." Afghanistan needs a force that is "light but as effective as heavy forces," he added, and should include tanks, and an infantry combat vehicle—protected mobility with some firepower.[135]

ANA Structure and Organization

In contrast to the post-war Iraqi army, which was built from the ground up starting with small units, the ANA has been built from the top down, starting with headquarters leadership and staff, and then gradually fielding units under those headquarters.

As of the end of 2009, the ANA had five ground forces Corps Headquarters—the 201st Corps in Kabul, the 203rd Corps in Gardez in the east, the 205th Corps in Kandahar in the south, the 207th Corps in Herat in the west, and the 209th Corps in Mazar-e Sharif in the north. Under those Corps headquarters, the ANA had 19 brigade headquarters, and 87 "kandak" (battalion) headquarters.[136] As of January 2009, according to ISAF officials, the ANA had 56 kandaks capable of battalion-level operations.[137]

ANA "Corps" follow the European model, in which a Corps is a two-star headquarters, whose subordinate units are brigades—much like a U.S. Army Division. The five ANA Corps areas of

---

[134] ANA Corps Commanding Generals, Interviews, Kandahar and Mazar-e-Sharif, Afghanistan, November 2008.

[135] Minister of Defense of Afghanistan Abdul Rahim Wardak, Interview, Kabul, Afghanistan, November 2008.

[136] See http://www.mod.gov.af, which calls itself the "website of the Afghan National Army."

[137] "Metrics Brief 2007-2008," International Security Assistance Force, January 2009.

responsibility (AOR), like the ISAF Regional Commands, are situated in the center, east, south, west, and north, but the ISAF and ANA boundaries do not completely correspond.

ANA Operations and Capabilities

Since the end of 2008, all ANA Corps were engaging regularly in combined operations with ISAF counterparts. The overall percentage of deliberate combined operations that were ANA-led had increased from 49%, in the period from October to December 2007, to 62% in the period from July to September 2008. The extent of ANA leadership of such operations varied significantly, however, among ISAF Regional Commands, from ANA leadership of 23% of combined deliberate operations in RC-South, to 43% in RC-North, to 79% in RC-East, and 86% in RC-West. U.S. officials responsible for training estimated that the disparities might have more to do with variations in the coalition-Afghan partnerships, from region to region, than with variations in the capabilities of the ANA Corps or security conditions in the various AORs.[138]

In qualitative terms, ISAF officials note that ANA operational capabilities have grown markedly. For example, in June 2008, following a prison break in Kandahar, initiated by a suicide bomber, the ANA deployed more than 1,000 soldiers south from Kabul, providing over half of the air lift required to transport them, within 24 hours. RC-East officials noted in November 2008 that in the previous month, they had participated in 35 combined "air assault" missions with the ANA, most of them ANA-led. In one mid-November action in eastern Afghanistan, for example, a combined ANA, ISAF and Afghan police force air assaulted into an area to be cleared. There, the Afghan police knocked on the doors, the ANA provided the inner cordon, and ISAF forces provided an outer cordon.[139]

Meanwhile, coalition special operations forces are helping the ANA develop elite "commando" kandaks. In theory, the commando forces would be capable of working with coalition counterparts on high-value targeting lists, and also of playing key roles in broader ANSF COIN operations.[140]

ANA as a National Institution

A number of observers have suggested that the ANA may be Afghanistan's only truly "national" institution. The outgoing head of CSTC-A noted that by late 2008 that the ANA was "very integrated." In the immediate post-Taliban years, ethnic Tajiks and Uzbeks—strongly represented in the Northern Alliance—predominated in Afghanistan's fledgling army, at the expense of ethnic Pashtuns. But as of the end of 2008, the ANA ethnic balance more closely corresponded to that of the population of Afghanistan—Tajiks, about 27% of the population, accounted for between 30 and 40% of the ANA, while Pashtuns, 42% of the population, made up 41% of the ANA. One caveat is that ethnic balance may not always correspond to geographic balance—for example, instead of recruiting Pashtuns from former Taliban stronghold areas in southern Afghanistan, the ANA may look to Pashtun communities in other parts of the country to achieve balance.[141]

---

[138] CSTC-A officials, Interviews, Kabul, Afghanistan, November 2008.

[139] ISAF officials, Interviews, Kabul, Bagram, and Khowst Province, Afghanistan, November 2008.

[140] CSTC-A officials, Interviews, Kabul, Afghanistan, November 2008; and see Gordon Lubold, "Americans Build Elite Afghan Commando Force," *Christian Science Monitor,* May 1, 2008.

[141] MG Robert Cone, other CSTC-A officials, Interviews, Kabul, Afghanistan, November 2008.

Meanwhile, Minister of Defense Wardak underscores that the ANA is well-regarded by the Afghan population.[142] This claim was supported by the results of a major survey of popular opinion conducted in 2008, under the auspices of the Asia Foundation, which identified the ANA as the public institution enjoying the highest level of public confidence in Afghanistan.[143]

Key Challenges to ANA Development

While ANA operational capabilities, by all accounts, continue to grow, the Army continues to contend with critical gaps and challenges. Like the Iraqi Army, the ANA lacks sufficient enablers, including logistics; intelligence, surveillance and reconnaissance (ISR); and air capabilities such as close air support (CAS). It continues to rely on U.S. and coalition forces for such support. In addition, the ANA faces a significant demographic gap, of personnel between the ages of 35 and 55, the legacy of Afghanistan's recent history of warfare. While the ANA can draw on its "older" personnel now to serve in leadership capacities, it will effectively take a generation to fully train and prepare the next contingent of ANA senior leaders. Further, the ANA—like Afghan society as a whole—suffers from a ravaged supply of Afghan human capital. Since a significant majority of new recruits are illiterate, ANA training relies on methodologies that do not utilize written language; and a number of literacy instruction opportunities are available.

Afghan National Army Air Corps (ANAAC)

The Afghan National Army Air Corps (ANAAC), effectively Afghanistan's air force, is organizationally part of the ANA and is considered its 6th Corps. Afghanistan has an independent air force tradition dating back to 1924—by the 1980's, after several periods of substantial Soviet assistance, Afghanistan had built a rather formidable air force. During the Taliban era, Pakistan assumed the foreign patronage role. During the war in 2001 that ousted the Taliban, Afghanistan's fleet was largely destroyed. Years of flying experience left the Afghans some human capital to draw on, in building a post-Taliban air force—although the current average age of its pilots, 44.7 years, is approximately the average life expectancy for Afghan males.

The ANAAC is trained and mentored by the Combined Air Power Transition Force (CAPTF), part of the CSTC-A. The CAPTF describes its ambitious goals for the ANAAC this way: "The ANAAC will be focused on the unique demands of Afghanistan but will also be modern, interoperable and sustainable, and integrated with the ANSF, capable of joint and combined operations...."[144]

CAPTF officials note that ANAAC development is proceeding in stages, based on agreements with ANSF leadership, with an initial emphasis on contributing to the COIN fight, first of all through air mobility. Afghanistan's unforgiving terrain and dearth of sufficient highway and rail

---

[142] Minister of Defense of Afghanistan Abdul Rahim Wardak, Interview, Kabul, Afghanistan, November 2008.

[143] *Afghanistan in 2008: A Survey of the Afghan People,* The Asia Foundation, 2008, p.25, available at http://asiafoundation.org/country/afghanistan/2008-poll.php. Other public institutions considered included the media, NGOs, national, provincial and local governing bodies, and community organizations. In the survey, 89% of respondents agreed that the ANA is "honest and fair with the Afghan people" (48% strongly agreed, 41% somewhat agreed), and 89% of respondents agreed that the "ANA helps improve security" (51% strongly agreed, and 35% somewhat agreed). This apparent high regard was not unqualified; 55% of respondents agreed that the "ANA is unprofessional and poorly trained" (18% strongly agreed, and 37% somewhat agreed), see p.35.

[144] CAPTF officials, Interviews, Kabul, Afghanistan, November 2008.

transportation make the ability to move troops and supplies absolutely critical. Later—in the period between FY2011 and FY2015—it is expected that the ANAAC will begin to acquire limited attack and ISR capabilities. Sometime thereafter, CAPTF officials note, the ANAAC might begin to build external defense capabilities, including air interdiction, but that is not a current focus. That timeline reportedly sits uneasily with some "legacy" Afghan fighter pilots, eager to rebuild the air force they once knew.[145]

As of October 2009, the ANAAC included 187 pilots, and the Afghan fleet comprised 29 rotary-winged and 10 fixed-wing aircraft. (20 Mi-17 and 9 Mi-35 helicopters; 5 AN-32 and 1 AN-26, 2 C-27 transport aircraft; and 2 L-39 "Albatros" jet trainer aircraft.) The current fleet, and the donations expected in the near term, almost are all of Soviet-bloc origin—CAPTF officials note that the first priority was to acquire early capability by capitalizing on aircraft familiar to the Afghans. Plans call for shifting the fleet's orientation away from former Soviet technology in future acquisitions, including fixed-wing cargo aircraft.[146]

By the end of 2008, the ANAAC was making substantial contributions to Afghan and coalition COIN efforts. In October 2008, the ANAAC set new records by transporting 9,000 passengers and 51 tons of cargo, and by flying 908 sorties. At the beginning of 2008, according to CAPTF officials, ISAF met 90% of ANA transport requirements for cargo and passengers, but by November, the ANAAC was meeting 90% of the requirement.[147]

Afghan National Police

The Afghan National Police (ANP) are Afghanistan's civilian security forces, which fall under the Ministry of the Interior. The ANP includes several distinct forces: the Afghan Uniform Police (AUP), responsible for general policing; the Afghan National Civil Order Police (ANCOP), a specialized police force that provides quick reaction forces; the Afghan Border Police (ABP), which provides law enforcement at Afghanistan's borders and entry points; and the Counternarcotics Police of Afghanistan (CNPA), which provides law enforcement support for reducing narcotics production and distribution.[148]

According to ANP officials, the ANP are being developed as a paramilitary force to contribute to the counterinsurgency effort by joining the ANA in COIN operations, and by protecting the population after the ANA "clears." As of October 2009, the ANP included approximately 90,100 assigned personnel.[149] The Bonn Agreement established a target ANP endstrength of 62,000; the current target endstrength is 96,800.

---

[145] CAPTF officials, Interviews, Kabul, Afghanistan, November 2008.

[146]. NATO Factsheet, "Facts and Figures: Afghan National Army," Media Operations Centre, NATO HQ, Brussels, Belgium, October 2009.

[147] CAPTF officials, Interviews, Kabul, Afghanistan, November 2008.

[148] See Department of Defense, United States Plan for Sustaining the Afghanistan National Security Forces, June 2008, p.21, available at http://www.defenselink.mil/pubs/
united_states_plan_for_sustaining_the_afghanistan_national_security_forces_1231.pdf.

[149] "Command Changes Hands for Afghan Security Forces Training," *American Forces Press Service*, December 22, 2008.

Police Corruption

The most commonly expressed concern of Afghan and international senior officials about the ANP is that they are not merely incompetent but also corrupt.[150] Some observers charge that such corruption is more than an obstacle to a job well done, in that it also alienates the population—the center of gravity in COIN—who may grow to see the Taliban as no worse than equally abusive civilian authorities.[151] Curiously, a major recent survey of Afghan popular opinion indicated that the ANP is the second most highly regarded public institution, after the ANA.[152]

Focused District Development

To address the problem, GIRoA and coalition forces launched the Focused District Development (FDD) initiative to retrain and reform local AUP forces, district-by-district. In the FDD program, the AUP are pulled out of a given district and sent to an intensive training course. Highly skilled ANCOP forces fill in, during their absence. After the AUP return, in order to reinforce their new skills, they operate under the tactical overwatch of, and then with mentoring by, coalition forces. As of January 2009, the AUP in 52 districts were undergoing the FDD process.[153] Coalition officials assess that FDD is generally successful, in that fewer violations by the AUP are reported after the training.

Some observers, including senior officials from international organizations, have charged that the program is not comprehensive enough to be effective. "Taking thugs away for a few weeks," one official observed, "just gives you better-trained thugs."[154]

Some outside observers, in turn, noting the urgent need for more and better policing on the streets of Afghanistan, have pushed for accelerated recruitment and fielding of weapons and equipment to the Afghan police. Coalition officials caution, however, that the reform process will take time, since the aim is a fundamental cultural shift. Providing gear, they argue, especially weapons, to "unreformed" districts, without proper accountability, would likely prove counterproductive.[155]

---

[150] General David McKiernan, Atlantic Council, Washington, DC, November 18, 2008, transcript available at http://www.acus.org/event_blog/general-david-d-mckiernan-speaks-councils-commanders-series/transcript. ISAF officials, Interviews, Kabul, Kandahar, Bagram, Afghanistan, November 2008.

[151] See Sarah Chayes, "Clean Up the Afghan Government, and the Taliban Will Fade Away," *Washington Post*, December 14, 2008. The author lives in Kandahar and runs an Afghan cooperative. She argues: "Now, Afghans are suffering so acutely that they hardly feel the difference between Taliban depredations and those of their own government." She quotes one local resident of Kandahar as saying: "The Taliban shake us down at night, and the government shakes us down in the daytime."

[152] *Afghanistan in 2008 - A Survey of the Afghan People*, The Asia Foundation, 2008, p.25, available at http://asiafoundation.org/country/afghanistan/2008-poll.php. In the survey, 80% of respondents agreed that the "ANP is honest and fair with the Afghan people," (40% strongly, 40% somewhat); while 80% agreed that the "ANP helps improve security" (40% strongly, 40% somewhat). At the same time, 60% agreed that the "ANP is unprofessional and poorly trained" (22% strongly, 38% somewhat).

[153] "Metrics Brief 2007-2008," International Security Assistance Force, January 2009.

[154] International organization official, Interview, Kabul, Afghanistan, November 2008.

[155] Coalition officials, Interviews, Kabul, Afghanistan, November 2008.

Afghan Border Police

By many accounts, the Afghan Border Police (ABP) may be beset by even greater incompetence and corruption than their AUP counterparts. To counteract these trends, GIRoA, working with coalition counterparts, launched the Focused Border Development (FBD) program, similar to the AUP's FDD. The courses are conducted by U.S. private security contractors—Blackwater and DynCorp. The retraining also includes arming the ABP with heavier weapons, including Soviet-origin DShK heavy machine guns.[156]

The FBD initiative, like FDD, relies on follow-up mentoring by coalition forces, after the completion of the formal training sessions. Those mentorship responsibilities are assigned to ISAF battlespace owners. As the outgoing head of CSTC-A observed, FBD is possible "because the 101st is helping me and giving me assets."[157]

Coalition and Afghan officials readily acknowledge the great challenge of securing Afghanistan's borders. Afghanistan has nearly 3,500 miles of borders, primarily in difficult, remote, mountainous terrain. Minister of Defense Wardak flatly observed, "We will never be able to secure the whole border."[158] Protecting the borders, some officials suggest, may require not only trained and professional ABP personnel stationed along the border, but also additional aerial reconnaissance and quick response forces.

Command and Control

Command and control arrangements for the ANSF have been adapted to current COIN efforts, which require "joint" action by multiple Afghan forces together with coalition counterparts. The Ministry of Defense and the Ministry of the Interior maintain formal command authority over their own forces—the ANA and the ANP, respectively.

To facilitate coordination, GIRoA created a series of Operations Coordination Commands, at the regional (OCC-R) and provincial (OCC-P) levels. There are 6 OCC-R's, one in each of the five ISAF Regional Commands, and one for Kabul city; and 34 OCC-P's are being established. OCC's at both levels are physical (not virtual) facilities that facilitate monitoring and coordination of operational and tactical-level operations.

OCC's include representatives from the ANA; the ANP; and the National Directorate of Security (NDS), Afghanistan's intelligence service. ISAF and CSTC-A provide mentoring. The command relationships among the participating organizations are purely "coordination," not "command." For example, as contingencies arise, OCC members provide direct conduits of information with their respective organizations—OCC-P members reach out to ANA brigades and ANP provincial command centers; while OCC-R members reach out to ANA Corps and ANP regional command centers. OCC-P's do not report to OCC-R's, and there is no national-level analogue. The ANA serves as the "lead agency" for OCC's, although OCC's may be physically located in police facilities.

---

[156] "CJTF-101 Campaign Update" slides, November 2008.

[157] MG Robert Cone, Interview, Kabul, Afghanistan, November 2008.

[158] Minister of Defense of Afghanistan Abdul Rahim Wardak, Interview, Kabul, Afghanistan, November 2008.

Looking to the future, some observers have wondered how appropriate the OCC construct will prove to be for a "post-COIN" context when, for example, the focus of the ANA shifts from domestic to external concerns. A future transition might not prove especially difficult, since the OCC coordination relationships complement but do not replace the formal service command relationships.[159]

Training the ANSF

Since its inception, the international ANSF training effort has been characterized by multiple initiatives adopting sometimes divergent approaches, with a general trend toward greater unity of effort, and a stronger U.S. leadership role, over time.[160] Secretary of State Clinton has underscored President Obama's statement "that we must focus more attention and resources on training the Afghan Security Forces."[161]

Background and Organization of the Training Effort

The December 2001 Bonn Conference recognized the need for the international community to help the fledgling Afghan authorities with "the establishment and training of new Afghan security and armed forces." In early 2002, broad agreement was reach on a model in which individual "lead nations" would assume primary responsibility to coordinate international assistance in five different areas of security—these included placing ANA development under U.S. leadership, and police sector development under German leadership. The 2006 Afghanistan Compact transferred formal "lead" responsibility to GIRoA.

In 2002, to execute its "lead nation" role, the United States created the Office of Military Cooperation-Afghanistan (OMC-A) to train the ANA. In 2002, to supplement German efforts, the U.S. government launched a police training initiative, led by the Department of State's Bureau of International Narcotics and Law Enforcement Affairs (INL), through U.S. Embassy Kabul, with contractor support. In 2005, the U.S. government restructured its ANSF training efforts, shifting

---

[159] The inter-service coordination arrangements in Afghanistan differ from those in Iraq, also designed for the exigencies of a counterinsurgency effort, where provincially-based "Operations Commands" bring together multiple Iraqi security forces under the formal command of the head of each Operations Command. Those arrangements may prove more difficult to rationalize, for a future post-COIN environment, than the OCC's in Afghanistan.

[160] U.S. government funding support to the ANSF has not followed a smooth trajectory to date. In FY2006, Congress appropriated approximately $1.9 billion for the Afghan Security Forces Fund, and in FY2007 – meeting DOD's request based on the need to accelerate Afghan ground forces training and equipping – $7.4 billion. In FY2008, Congress appropriated approximately $2.7 billion for the Fund, again meeting DOD's request, which was based on the premise of building on the ANSF acceleration enabled by the FY2007 appropriations. For FY2009, DOD requested an increase – $3.7 billion – in its Global War on Terror bridge request, submitted in May 2008, of which Congress provided $2 billion. See CRS Report RL33110, *The Cost of Iraq, Afghanistan, and Other Global War on Terror Operations Since 9/11*, by Amy Belasco. See also Department of Defense, "FY 2007 Emergency Supplemental Request for the Global War on Terror," February 2007, available at http://www.defenselink.mil/comptroller/Docs/ FY2007_Emergency_Supplemental_Request_for_the_GWOT.pdf; Department of Defense, "FY 2008 Global War on Terror Request," February 2007, available at http://www.defenselink.mil/comptroller/Docs/ FY2008_February_Global_War_On_Terror_Request.pdf; and Department of Defense, "Fiscal Year 2009 Global War on Terror Bridge Request," May 2008, available at http://www.defenselink.mil/comptroller/defbudget/fy2009/ Supplemental/FY2009_Global_War_On_Terror_Bridge_Request.pdf.

[161] See the replies to questions for the record, submitted by Secretary of State nominee Hillary Clinton to the Senate Foreign Relations Committee (SFRC), for her January 13, 2009, confirmation hearing, available at http://www.foreignpolicy.com/files/KerryClintonQFRs.pdf.

---

responsibility for supporting Afghan police development to the Department of Defense, and renaming the OMC-A the Office of Security Cooperation-Afghanistan (OSC-A).[162] Early in 2007, when the U.S. three-star military headquarters, the Combined Forces Command-Afghanistan (CFC-A) was deactivated, OSC-A was re-designated the Combined Security Transition Command-Afghanistan (CSTC-A), and assigned directly to US CENTCOM; CSTC-A was assigned to USFOR-A when that headquarters was established in 2008.

Training Teams

CSTC-A's primary mechanism for training and advising the ANSF is the use small teams that typically live and work with ANSF units. U.S. advisory teams working with the ANA—Embedded Training Teams (ETTs)—include between 12 and 20 personnel. ETTs work for CSTC-A but are under the operational command of U.S. battlespace owners during combined operations with the ANSF. Non-U.S. NATO advisory teams are known as Operational Mentor and Liaison Teams (OMLT). In theory, their functions are similar to those of the ETTs, but due to national caveats, there are great variations in the degree to which OMLTs participate in operations with their Afghan counterparts. Advisory teams working with the ANP are known as Police Mentoring Teams (PMTs).

Some officials in battlespace-owning units have argued that the quality of ETT and PMT personnel varies and that, as one official put it, "the ETTs are better suited to planning than execution."[163] In October 2006, the U.S. Army consolidated, at Fort Riley, Kansas, the pre-deployment training and preparation of U.S. Army, Navy and Air Force personnel for assignments as advisors to Afghan and Iraqi security forces; in October 2008, the Army announced that the program would shift to the Joint Readiness Training Center at Fort Polk, Louisiana.[164] One reason for some reported variation in the quality of U.S. advisors may be that they are selected on an individual basis and come from a wide variety of backgrounds that may or may not include extensive operational experience.

Mentoring the ANSF Leadership

In addition to tactical- and operational-level training, the coalition ANSF advisory effort also includes mentoring Afghan senior leaders—Ministers, senior ministry officials, and senior ANA and ANP commanders. ISAF and CSTC-A senior leaders invest considerable time in working closely with the senior leadership of the Defense and Interior Ministers, and of their regionally-based commands. President Karzai replaced the Minister of Interior in October 2008, a step favored by a number of senior U.S. and other international officials in Afghanistan, and widely

---

[162] In a 2008 report, regarding the establishment of the OSC-A, DOD noted: "Efforts prior to this time were not comprehensive and lacked both resources and unity of effort within the international community." See Department of Defense, *United States Plan for Sustaining the Afghanistan National Security Forces*, June 2008, p.21, available at http://www.defenselink.mil/pubs/
united_states_plan_for_sustaining_the_afghanistan_national_security_forces_1231.pdf. The OSC-A, like the OMC-A, reported to the U.S. military command in Afghanistan, but received policy guidance from the U.S. Chief of Mission, while contract management authority remained with State INL.

[163] ISAF and CSTC-A officials, Interviews, Kabul, Kandahar, Bagram, Afghanistan, November 2008.

[164] John Milburn, "Adviser Mission to Leave Fort Riley," *Army Times,* October 1, 2008. The U.S. Marine Corps has its own program for preparing Marines for advisory roles.

viewed as an effort to curb corruption.[165] The coalition "advisory" role is strong—Afghan regional commanders regularly seek coalition support, and advocacy with their respective ministries, for identified requirements. The fundamental challenge is building institutional capacity—including leadership ability, physical infrastructure, effective systems, and trained and competent human resources.

Unit Partnering

In Iraq, the Iraqi security forces (ISF) training and advisory effort relied on two complementary approaches, embedded teams and "unit partnering." Unit partnering involved matching a full coalition unit with an Iraqi counterpart of equal or greater seniority in a mentoring relationship. Multi-National Corps-Iraq directed the use of such partnerships where appropriate. Those relationships, in the words of U.S. commanders in Iraq, provided the opportunity to "show, rather than tell"—to provide visible examples of a competent unit and staff in action.

In Afghanistan in late 2008, the use of unit partnering was more ad hoc, and more contentious. Overall, unit partnering was less widespread than in Iraq, a natural consequence of a far lighter coalition footprint, since unit partnering requires available, locally-based units of appropriate size. Nevertheless, battlespace-owning U.S. units underscored the importance of such partnerships—as one commander noted, "ANSF capacity-building is our main effort, and we accept some risk in our operational capabilities to focus on this." For example, one U.S. brigade-sized Task Force sends its tactical command post including key brigade staff, for two weeks every month, to co-locate and partner with the nearest ANA Corps headquarters. Its Military Police (MP) battalion headquarters staff, in turn, work closely with the ANP Regional Command Center.

Further, the ANP re-training effort, for both AUP and ABP, requires substantial follow-up in the form of mentoring. Battlespace-owning units were tasked to establish and maintain those mentoring partnerships—a form of unit partnering—with the "reformed" ANP.[166]

At the same time, in late 2008, senior Afghan and CSTC-A officials evinced an antipathy toward the concept of unit partnering. Minister of Defense Wardak argued forcefully: "There is some talk that we should do partnering, but I am against it—our units are standing on their own feet. I will try very hard to push against this partnering. If they have partner units, they would lose their ability to learn and operate independently."[167] CSTC-A officials argued, similarly, that ANSF units tended to perform less well when partnered with coalition units, and that advisory teams were more effective than "partners" in encouraging the ANSF to take initiative.[168]

Community and Tribal Outreach

Afghan and ISAF officials have undertaken a new community outreach program, sometimes called the "community guard program," designed to take a bottom-up, community-based approach to security.[169] The premise is that neither international forces nor the ANSF have

---

[165] John F. Burns, "Afghan President, Pressured, Reshuffles Cabinet," *The New York Times*, October 11, 2008.

[166] Task Force Currahee, Interviews, Khowst Province, Afghanistan, November 2008.

[167] Minister of Defense of Afghanistan Abdul Rahim Wardak, Interview, Kabul, Afghanistan, November 2008.

[168] CSTC-A officials, Interviews, Kabul, Afghanistan, November 2008.

[169] General David McKiernan, Atlantic Council, Washington, DC, November 18, 2008, transcript available at (continued...)

---

sufficient numbers to provide full population security, and are not likely to have them in the near future, even with expected increases in ISAF and ANSF troop strength. Minister of Defense Wardak has stated, "There is still a big gap between forces available, and the space to secure, so we need help."[170]

In Afghanistan, local community leaders are often tribal leaders, and local community structure is intimately linked with tribal structure, though not necessarily clearly or consistently. Observers describe tribal bonds as "pragmatic, localized allegiances," which may have been shaped over time by migration, competition for resources, reallocation of land rights as rewards for services, and links to the narcotics trade. While residents of several isolated valleys may all belong to the same tribe, their fiercest rivalries may be with fellow tribesmen in an adjacent valley. Fostering local community support for security initiatives generally involves working with tribal leaders, among others, but given Afghanistan's complex tribal affiliations, the risk of "getting it wrong" is relatively high.[171]

The community guard program attempts to avoid "getting it wrong" by focusing on the concept of "community outreach," rather than "tribal outreach." The initiative began with the recognition of the need to protect Highway 1, the key artery running south from Kabul to Kandahar and the site of escalating insurgent attacks in mid-to-late 2008. The program was expected to begin with a pilot project in Wardak and Logar provinces, just south of Kabul. Muhammad Halim Fidai, Governor of Wardak province, was quoted as saying: "We don't have enough police to keep the Taliban out of these villages and we don't have time to train more police—we have to fill the gap now."[172]

In the program, each local "community"—including all relevant tribes—would select representatives to a shura; the shura, in turn, would select project participants to help provide security, for example through neighborhood watch efforts and guarding fixed sites. One goal, U.S. officials noted, is that local residents adopt a "not in my village" attitude toward insurgents and criminals.[173]

Funding for the program would be provided by U.S. CERP funds; this funding would not cover arming participants. U.S. accountability requirements mandate formal U.S. oversight, but additional Afghan oversight would be provided by both on-site ANSF representatives, and the moral authority of the community shura. The goal—as U.S. Ambassador William Wood stated—is "to empower locals, both local governance and tribal structures, to make them work for themselves."[174] "The idea," as Minister of Defense Wardak expressed it, "is to bridge the gap between the government and the people, and to make the people feel responsible."[175]

(...continued)

http://www.acus.org/event_blog/general-david-d-mckiernan-speaks-councils-commanders-series/transcript; and "U.S. Backs Plan for Engaging Afghan Tribes," *Radio Free Europe Radio Liberty*, December 30, 2008.

[170] Minister of Defense of Afghanistan Abdul Rahim Wardak, Interview, Kabul, Afghanistan, November 2008.

[171] ISAF, RC-South officials, and western diplomats, Interviews, Kabul, Afghanistan, November 2008.

[172] Jon Boone, "Afghans Fear U.S. Plan to Rearm Villages," *Financial Times*, January 12, 2009.

[173] ISAF officials, Interviews, Kabul, Afghanistan, November 2008.

[174] Ambassador William Wood, Interview, Kabul, Afghanistan, November 2008.

[175] Minister of Defense of Afghanistan Abdul Rahim Wardak, Interview, Kabul, Afghanistan, November 2008. He added, "If you make a community responsible, and you given them the feeling that they are sharing in that responsibility, then they will die for it."

The initiative draws to some extent on the model of "arbakai"—a traditional Pashtun institution, in which a tribally-based auxiliary force is formed to defend a village and its surrounding area on a temporary basis. That familiar association may help smooth the introduction of community outreach, but it also raises concerns in some quarters that the program might reignite and facilitate local warlordism.[176]

Minister of Defense Wardak is reportedly particularly concerned about the danger of a return to the chaos of the early 1990's civil war. He stated in late 2008 that the new program must not re-arm anyone—"we should not create new warlords or reinforce old ones."[177] U.S. officials quoted a senior ANA commander as saying, reflecting cautiously on the initiative, "The army and police serve a nation, but a militia serves a man."[178]

The program must also overcome the legacy of similar and more recent initiatives to generate security at the local level. The Afghan National Auxiliary Police program was created in 2006, amidst some controversy, as a stop-gap measure in southern Afghanistan. The locally-recruited force, including many who previously worked for warlords, had an approved size of 11,271. Recruits were given ten days of training, and members received the same salaries as regular ANP street cops—$70 per month.[179] A number of practitioners and observers argued that the training was insufficient to produce a credible security force. At the time, the head of CSTC-A called the program "an attempt to take short-cuts," and its participants "a bunch of thugs," and more recently, an RC-East senior official concluded that they "went brigand."[180] By late 2008, the program had been completely dismantled.

Reconciliation

Military theorists and practitioners contend that war is a contest over the terms of an ultimate political settlement. In Afghanistan, both GIRoA and the various insurgent groups are contending to set the conditions for a final settlement.

In an early preview of a possible end game for the war in Afghanistan, in late 2008 a rhetoric of "reconciliation" with the Taliban and other insurgents gained momentum. Practitioners and observers have used the word "reconciliation" to refer to two different kinds of efforts in Afghanistan—lower-level efforts to co-opt the fence-sitters and hired guns, and higher-level negotiations aimed at bringing senior leaders in from the cold.

Some refer to the first group as "small-t taliban," those driven by poverty, lack of jobs and other prospects, and general disaffection, who provide their services to insurgent leaders for some price.[181] The purpose of reconciliation efforts would be to "peel them off" from the hardcore

[176] RC-East official, Interview, Bagram, Afghanistan, November 2008.

[177] Minister of Defense of Afghanistan Abdul Rahim Wardak, Interview, Kabul, Afghanistan, November 2008.

[178] RC-East official, Interview, Bagram, Afghanistan, November 2008.

[179] See Andrew Wilder, "Cops or Robbers? The Struggle to Reform the Afghan National Police," *Afghanistan Research and Evaluation Unit,* July 2007.

[180] See Jerome Starkey, "US attacks UK plan to arm Afghan militias," *The Independent,* January 14, 2008; and Murray Brewster, "NATO Disbands Afghan Auxiliary Police," *Edmonton Sun,* May 15, 2008; MG Robert Cone, Interview, Kabul, Afghanistan, November 2008; RC-East official, Interview, Bagram, Afghanistan, November 2008.

[181] General David McKiernan, Interview, Kabul, Afghanistan, November 2008. See also General David McKiernan, Atlantic Council, Washington, DC, November 18, 2008, transcript available at http://www.acus.org/event_blog/ (continued...)

insurgency, perhaps through some combination of economic incentives, opportunities for political participation, and removal from targeting lists. To be clear, while U.S. commanders support such "reconciliation," they stress that any such initiatives would be GIRoA—not ISAF or U.S.—efforts.

The second category of reconciliation includes outreach to, and possibly negotiations with, senior leaders of the Taliban and other insurgent groups. President Karzai has stated publicly that efforts to encourage the Saudis to broker contacts have been ongoing for several years, but so far without results.[182] The Saudis have also reportedly facilitated contact with representatives of Gulbuddin Hekmatyar and his HiG organization.[183]

For its part, the Taliban has reportedly named conditions that must be met before it would agree to enter any direct talks. These include the withdrawal of all international forces from Afghanistan, immunity of Taliban leaders from targeting by the ANSF, and the ability to retain their weapons. According to U.S. senior officials, such demands would contradict GIRoA principles—for example, that all Afghan citizens must renounce violence and accept the Constitution—and U.S. government views.[184]

One further challenge, according to many practitioners and observers, is that despite suffering some tactical-level set-backs, the Taliban leadership appears to feel confident, free to approach any talks from a position of strength. One senior UK official stressed that if negotiations took place today, the Taliban would make unrealistic demands, and he estimated that we are "many months if not years from the end game." He added, "there's no 'quick fix' through reconciliation."[185] Some ISAF officials add that Taliban leaders may be under some pressure from al Qaeda not to participate in negotiations.[186]

Counternarcotics[187]

The Narcotics Problem

One of the things that make the conflict in Afghanistan so intractable is the close linkage between the Afghan insurgency and narcotics. The United Nations Office on Drugs and Crime reported that "warlords, drug lords, and insurgents" collect a tax on the cultivation, transportation and processing of opium poppy—taxes that amounted to "almost $500 million in 2008."[188] The twin counternarcotics (CN) and counterinsurgency challenge is most evident in Helmand province in

---

(...continued)

general-david-d-mckiernan-speaks-councils-commanders-series/transcript.

[182] See John F. Burns, "Karzai Sought Saudi Help With Taliban," *The New York Times*, October 1, 2008; and Anand Gopal, "No Afghan-Taliban Peace Talks for Now," *Christian Science Monitor*, October 9, 2008.

[183] Kim Sengupta, "Secret Saudi Dinner, Karzai's Brother and the Taliban," *The Independent,* October 8, 2008.

[184] Senior U.S. officials, Interviews, Kabul, Afghanistan, November 2008; and see John F. Burns, "Karzai Sought Saudi Help With Taliban," *The New York Times*, October 1, 2008.

[185] UK official, Interview, Kabul, Afghanistan, November 2008.

[186] ISAF officials, Interviews, Kabul, Afghanistan, November 2008.

[187] For a detailed discussion, see CRS Report RL32686, *Afghanistan: Narcotics and U.S. Policy*, by Christopher M. Blanchard.

[188] *Afghanistan Opium Survey 2008*, United Nations Office on Drugs and Crime, November 2008.

southern Afghanistan, which is responsible for about two-thirds of Afghan opium production and provides a base of operations for some Taliban insurgents.

Narcotics are big business in Afghanistan—with a climate conducive to cultivation, an absence of readily available economic alternatives such as the infrastructure for bringing legitimate crops to market, and permeable borders with neighboring states. Senior U.S. officials note the reluctance of many Afghan officials to challenge the narcotics industry because its tentacles are so deeply entwined with Afghan governing structures at all levels. Furthermore, Afghanistan still lacks the robust judicial system that would be necessary to prosecute offenders.

Counternarcotics Approaches

The government of Afghanistan and its international partners have produced no shortage of strategies designed to address Afghanistan's narcotics problem. The current GIRoA plan is the Afghan National Drug Control Strategy, issued in January 2006; a previous version was issued in May 2003.[189] In early 2002, as a follow-on to the Bonn Agreement, the United Kingdom assumed "lead nation" responsibility for coordinating international counternarcotics (CN) efforts; that lead responsibility shifted to GIRoA under the 2006 Afghanistan Compact.

The first premise of the CN effort is the illegality of narcotics. On January 17, 2002, President Karzai issued a decree banning the cultivation, production, abuse, and trafficking of narcotic drugs. Key Afghan CN organizations include the Afghan Special Narcotics Force (or "Task Force 333"), a paramilitary force created in late 2003 to conduct raids; the Counternarcotics Police of Afghanistan, which investigates and helps target networks; an eradication force that physically carries out eradication; and a CN Criminal Justice Task Force created in early 2005 to expedite CN cases through the fledgling criminal justice system. GIRoA has sought the close cooperation of provincial Governors in its CN efforts. "Governor-led eradication" (GLE) efforts encourage Governors to cooperate by offering them control over the eradication process, and providing them rewards in the form of resources from the central government. Critics have suggested that GLE efforts may selectively target political rivals or small-scale cultivators, while avoiding confrontation with powerful larger-scale producers. In 2006, GIRoA launched the Good Performers Initiative to reward provinces for reducing poppy cultivation.

To support the Afghan CN strategy, and also in an attempt to shape it, the U.S. government issued its own U.S. Counternarcotics Strategy for Afghanistan, in August 2007. While GIRoA has tended to favor negotiated eradication—including its collaboration with provincial Governors—the U.S. government has supported the more forceful approach of centralized and enforced GIRoA-led "non-negotiated forced eradication."[190]

Since assuming command of ISAF, U.S. commanders have lobbied for a more active NATO role in counternarcotics, including the ability for ISAF forces to target narcotics labs. At an informal meeting of NATO Ministers of Defense, held in Budapest in October 2008, the Allies agreed to stretch the CN role that ISAF can play without changing its formal mandate. After the meeting, NATO Secretary-General Jaap de Hoop Scheffer announced that "under the existing operational

---

[189] Government of Afghanistan, *Afghan National Drug Control Strategy: An Updated Five-Year Strategy for Tackling the Illicit Drug Problem,* Islamic Republic of Afghanistan Ministry of Counter-Narcotics, Kabul, January 2006.

[190] Ambassador Thomas A. Schweich, Coordinator for Counternarcotics and Justice Reform in Afghanistan, *U.S. Counternarcotics Strategy for Afghanistan,* August 2007, see especially pp.5-6, and 48.

plan, ISAF can act in concert with the Afghans against facilities and facilitators supporting the insurgency, in the context of counternarcotics, subject to authorization of respective nations."[191] The following month, General McKiernan explained that there was no change to the rules of engagement—just a decision "to be more aggressive." He added, "Where I can make the connection between narcotics, personalities, or facilities, and the insurgency, then I can treat that as a military objective."[192] In December 2008, a senior ISAF official noted that GIRoA had already asked for ISAF's assistance several times, on the basis of the October 2008 policy update.[193]

Counternarcotics Results

Practitioners and outside experts differ concerning how best to evaluate the results of these counternarcotics efforts. Some simply point to poppy-free provinces—in particular Nangarhar in eastern Afghanistan along the Pakistani border—as successes, and credit a combination of various GIRoA eradication efforts. They suggest in particular the importance of local authorities in discouraging poppy planting. Other observers argue that global food prices may be a more important explanatory variable—in 2008, opium prices were down, while wheat prices, due to a widespread drought, were up, possibly affecting the decision calculus of many planters. They underscore the importance of cultivation trends over time, rather than one-time developments, as better indicators of program effectiveness. Two analysts from this school of thought have argued: "Sustainable reductions in opium poppy cultivation will only be achieved by a wider process of improved security, economic growth and governance."[194]

Capacity-Building as Part of COIN in Afghanistan

According to civilian and military practitioners, the three pillars of the counterinsurgency effort in Afghanistan—security, governance, and development—are inseparably linked. As former advisor to both GIRoA and ISAF Clare Lockhart asserts, "A country is not stable until it has a functioning state that performs key functions for its citizens."[195] International military forces in Afghanistan lead the security line of operation, and also play strong supporting roles in the other two fields, governance and development, particularly at the provincial and local levels where their footprint is much greater than that of civilian counterparts.[196]

---

[191] NATO press release, October 10, 2008, available at http://www.nato.int/docu/update/2008/10-october/e1010b.html.

[192] General David McKiernan, Atlantic Council, Washington, DC, November 18, 2008, transcript available at http://www.acus.org/event_blog/general-david-d-mckiernan-speaks-councils-commanders-series/transcript.

[193] Dave Pugliese, "ISAF Commander Says Afghan Drug Lords to Be on 'Kill or Capture' Target List," *Ottawa Citizen*, December 23, 2008.

[194] David Mansfield and Adam Pain, "Counter-Narcotics in Afghanistan: The Failure of Success?" *Afghanistan Research and Evaluation Unit Briefing Paper Series,* December 2008, p.3.

[195] Clare Lockhart, "Learning from Experience," *Slate*, November 5, 2008.

[196] The 2006 COIN field manual states: "Political, social and economic programs are most commonly and appropriately associated with civilian organizations and expertise; however, effective implementation of these programs is more important than who performs the tasks. If adequate civilian capacity is not available, military forces fill the gap." Field Manual 3-24, *Counterinsurgency,* Headquarters, Department of the Army, December 2006, para. 2-5.

The Need for Capacity-Building

Practitioners and observers generally agree that improving the capacity of Afghan institutions is essential for making progress in all three lines of operation—security, governance and development. Many further stress that a critical component of capacity-building in Afghanistan is connecting the center to the regions. Popular support—active or passive—is essential to counterinsurgency, and local-level institutions, whether political officials or the ANSF, are often the most readily-available "face" of government. Local capacity, it is argued, should be competent, and should help connect the local population to a larger "Afghanistan."

One fundamental challenge to capacity-building in general is that Afghanistan's would-be work force was decimated by years of violence and repression, and generally lacks the skills, the professionalism, and often the literacy, to work in a post-Taliban polity or economy.

Some observers argue that the human capital problem was exacerbated by bad choices by the international community in the immediate aftermath of Taliban rule. Eager to place responsibility for leading Afghanistan in Afghan hands—and eager in some cases to focus primarily on the counter-terrorist mission—the international community, it is charged, failed to insist on high standards of experience or integrity in the selection of Afghan leaders at all levels. One ISAF official argued in late 2008, "We need a major housecleaning of GIRoA."[197]

Other observers have stressed that the international community, and particularly the U.S. government, further aggravates the human capital problem by supporting specific individuals, rather than impartially supporting the Afghan political process as a whole. Such approaches, it is argued, make it difficult to hold such officials accountable. Noting another ramification, NATO SCR Gentilini described such approaches by the U.S. government as "good but colonialist," because the U.S.-supported officials may be seen as U.S. pawns.[198]

A significant challenge to local-level capacity-building is that provincial Governors and district Administrators have very little formal authority, and they receive no budgets of their own from the central government. As one diplomat described it, in the absence of resources, Governors have to negotiate their authority with *de facto* local power-brokers, which compromises their efforts.[199]

Military Role and Perspectives on Capacity-Building

ISAF and U.S. military officials in Afghanistan acknowledge that their role in civilian capacity-building is a "supporting" one, but they stress the importance of their role in helping link together the various levels of government. With a footprint that extends through most of the country, and that includes a presence at the local as well as the national and regional levels, the military is well-placed to make such contributions.

For example, the mission statement of the 101st Airborne Division, once the nucleus of ISAF's RC-East, underscored the military's role in all three pillars of efforts. It stated that RC-East, in conjunction with GIRoA, ISAF and U.S. civilian agencies, "conducts full spectrum operations to

---

[197] ISAF official, Interview, Kabul, Afghanistan, November 2008.

[198] Ambassador Ferrnando Gentilini, Interview, Kabul, Afghanistan, November 2008.

[199] ISAF official, Interview, Kandahar, Afghanistan, November 2008.

develop Afghan national capability to secure its people, exercise capable governance, and develop a sustainable economy, while defeating terrorists and insurgents, in order to extend GIRoA authority and influence as the legitimate government of the Afghan people."[200]

A former U.S. brigade commander in eastern Afghanistan noted that his company commanders worked regularly with district-level officials, monitoring their efforts, and that this focus was important because "the cause of instability in Afghanistan is poor governance."[201]

In late 2008, a senior ISAF official explained that the military's role is to "facilitate" governance, which is "the long pole in the tent," and harder than either security or development. He added that squad and platoon leaders on the ground "regularly liaise with local Afghan officials." Their guidance is to work "bottom-up," to get information, to facilitate shuras, to connect district officials with representatives of Kabul-based ministries…and to follow up assiduously.[202]

Provincial Reconstruction Teams

Provincial Reconstructions Teams (PRT) in Afghanistan grew out of a U.S. military initiative in late 2002. In general, PRTs help Afghan provincial governments develop the capacity and capabilities to govern, provide security, ensure the rule of law, promote development, and meet the needs of the population.[203] The U.S.-led PRT in Zabul province, for example, succinctly states that its mandate is "to conduct civil-military operations in Zabul to extend the reach and legitimacy of GIRoA."[204] As ISAF's area of responsibility expanded geographically, it assumed responsibility for PRTs in each new area. As of early 2009, ISAF maintains 26 PRTs, each led by a single nation. PRT staff may include any combination of civilian and military personnel; the military components formally report to ISAF.

The U.S. government leads 12 of ISAF's 26 PRTs, 10 of them in RC-East, one in RC-South, and one in RC-West. PRTs do not currently cover all of Afghanistan's 34 provinces. In late 2008, some U.S. officials were considering possible future expansions, including creating two separate PRTs from the single entity currently responsible for Kapisa and Parwan provinces; establishing a PRT-like entity for Kabul city; and creating new PRTs in Dai Kundi and Nimroz provinces in RC-South.

U.S. PRTs are primarily military organizations, each led by a military officer—either an Air Force Lieutenant Colonel or a Navy Commander—who reports to the nearest U.S. battlespace owner. Typically, a PRT includes between 80 and 150 staff members, including one representative each from the Department of State, the Agency for International Development (AID), and the Department of Agriculture (USDA).

---

[200] "CJTF-101 Campaign Update" slides, November 2008.

[201] Ann Marlowe, "A Counterinsurgency Grows in Khowst," *Weekly Standard,* May 19, 2008. Colonel Marty Schweitzer led the 4th BCT, 82nd Airborne Division, in 6 provinces of RC-East.

[202] ISAF official, Interview, Kabul, Afghanistan, November 2008.

[203] For a current U.S. PRT mission statement, see "Fact Sheet: Making Afghanistan More Secure with Economic and Reconstruction Assistance," White House, September 26, 2008, available at http://www.whitehouse.gov/news/releases/2008/09/20080926-16.html.

[204] Zabul PRT officials, Interviews, Zabul province, Afghanistan, November 2008.

Practitioners and observers variously evaluate the successes of PRTs to date. Some argue that while PRTs have carried out useful work, they have not been resourced sufficiently to meet requirements. This may be particularly true for some Allies, for example Lithuania, that have fewer resources available in general for international assistance efforts.[205]

Others, including senior GIRoA officials, have argued that PRTs do not coordinate their efforts sufficiently with Afghan authorities. In November 2008, during a visit to Kabul by a U.N. Security Council delegation, President Karzai claimed that PRTs were setting up "parallel governments" in the countryside.[206] Other GIRoA officials reportedly express that many international resources channeled through PRTs are effectively "lost" amidst multiple layers of contractors and subcontractors, before they reach the Afghan people.[207]

Other U.S. Civilian Field Presence

In addition to the U.S. government civilian agency presence at PRTs, civilian representatives from the State Department, AID, and USDA also serve at U.S. "Task Forces"—division and brigade headquarters under ISAF. Typically, these civilians provide advisory support, in their respective fields of expertise, helping inform military decision-making and operations. U.S. commanders typically express strong enthusiasm for these partnerships.[208] In November 2008, a total of 60 U.S. civilians were serving in "field positions"—at PRTs and Task Forces.[209]

U.S. civilian experts work with battlespace-owning military units in another capacity, on Human Terrain Teams (HTT), established in Afghanistan in February 2007.[210] HTTs, recruited and employed by the U.S. Army, are small teams of social scientists, from various academic disciplines, who conduct deep anthropological fieldwork in order to understand and "map" demographic, social and economic dynamics. Their analysis, like the advice of the State, AID and USDA civilian advisors, helps inform military decision-making and operations. U.S. commanders praise the work of the HTTs as contributing directly to their understanding of the battlespace and some have noted that more HTTs—as much as one per district—would be welcome.[211] Their work, like that of servicemembers, entails risk—one member of the HTT in Khowst province, Afghanistan, was killed in May 2008 when his vehicle was struck by an improvised explosive device (IED).

At the same time, the deployment of HTTs has met with both criticism and complications. HTTs have been criticized, most frequently by the academic community, for "compromising" social

---

[205] The constraint of limited resources may also apply to U.S.-led PRTs. In late 2008, the Zabul PRT introduced a new ionizer-based water purification initiative – a scheme developed and proposed by an American Eagle Scout. While that Eagle Scout's contributions may be laudable, some suggest that PRTs ought to be able to draw on more readily available expertise.

[206] Associated Press, "Afghan President Complains U.S., NATO Aren't Succeeding," Foxnews.com, November 26, 2008.

[207] ISAF officials, and Minister of Defense of Afghanistan Abdul Rahim Wardak, Interviews, Kabul, Afghanistan, November 2008.

[208] RC-East, TF Currahee officials, Interviews, Bagram and Khowst province, Afghanistan, November 2008.

[209] Zabul PRT officials, Interviews, Zabul province, Afghanistan, November 2008.

[210] For information, see the Human Terrain System website, http://humanterrainsystem.army.mil/default.htm.

[211] RC-East and TF Currahee officials and HTT members, Interviews, Bagram and Khowst province, Afghanistan, November 2008. To be clear, HTT members state that they "do not do targeting."

---

science ethical standards.[212] In November 2008, an HTT member, Don Ayala, was charged with murder in connection with the killing of an Afghan man who had set a female HTT member on fire, in Kandahar province.[213]

Commanders Emergency Response Program (CERP)

Particularly in the absence of dedicated provincial or district budgets, U.S. commanders have made use of the Commanders Emergency Response Program (CERP), sponsored by the Department of Defense, to fund governance- and development-related projects. One U.S. commander recently called CERP "a surrogate for the government's failure to provide," and another stated, "If we didn't have CERP, we wouldn't be able to do anything."[214]

Since its inception, CERP has provided relatively unconstrained discretionary funds to military commanders on the ground, to meet relatively near-term needs. With far fewer U.S. forces—and thus fewer senior U.S. commanders entitled to spend CERP funds—Afghanistan has received less CERP funding to date than Iraq.

According to U.S. civilian and military officials, and some Afghan provincial officials, decisions about CERP funding allocation are typically based on Afghan priorities and informed by both U.S. civilian and military expertise. The top expenditure to date, by a significant margin, has been road-construction, viewed by Afghans and U.S. officials as critical to security, governance and development.

Agribusiness Development Teams

Supplementing the work of battlespace owners, their civilian advisors, and PRTs in eastern Afghanistan are Agribusiness Development Teams (ADT). ADTs are state-based Army National Guard (ARNG) teams that include "farmer soldiers" who have backgrounds in various facets of agribusiness. The ADTs draw on several decades of similar ARNG experience in Central America, and typically they leverage agricultural expertise from land grant universities in their home states. The teams include organic enablers that allow them to operate independently, including vehicles and force protection.

In 2008, the first ADT, from Missouri, deployed to newly poppy-free Nangarhar province, and the second ADT, from Texas, deployed to Ghazni province. Guardsmen and women from Indiana, Kansas, Kentucky, Nebraska, Oklahoma, and Tennessee have also been involved in the program.[215]

---

[212] See for example, Network of Concerned Anthropologists, "Anthropologists Up in Arms Over Pentagon's 'Human Terrain System' to Recruit Graduate Students to Serve in Iraq, Afghanistan: an interview with David Price," *Democracy Now*, December 13, 2007, available at http://www.democracynow.org/2007/12/13/ anthropologists_up_in_arms_over_pentagons.

[213] See Jeff Schogol, "DoD Contractor Charged in Death of Afghan Man," *Stars and Stripes,* November 22, 2008; and Jerry Markon, "Contractor Charged," *Washington Post*, November 20, 2008.

[214] RC-East and TF Currahee officials, Interviews, Bagram and Khowst province, Afghanistan, November 2008.

[215] RC-East and TF Currahee officials, Interviews, Bagram and Khowst provinces, Afghanistan, November 2008. See also Tom Vanden Brook, "Harvesting Ties with Afghanistan," *Army Times*, December 31, 2008.

A Civilian Surge?

Many practitioners and observers have suggested that the capacity-building challenges in Afghanistan may require additional international civilian expertise, as well as the effective integration of such expertise with military efforts.

ISAF commanders argue that a stronger commitment to build capacity is required, because it is governance, more than security or development, that is lagging in Afghanistan. RC-East Commanding General MG Schloesser has argued, "We need an interagency surge!"[216] Senior officials from other Allies within ISAF echo this argument—in November 2008, RC-North Commanding General, German Major General Weigt, argued that he needed "civilian advisory teams," as complements to the OMLTs and ETTs. "The main problem for me," he stated," is not security, but deficits in governance."[217]

Outside observers have also argued that the civilian capacity-building effort should be as robust as security capacity-building initiatives. State-building expert Sarah Chayes wrote in December 2008 that the problem of governance in Afghanistan is particularly acute. She argued, "Western governments should send experienced former mayors, district commissioners and water and health department officials to mentor Afghans in those roles."[218]

Some observers have suggested that Afghanistan might be a useful test case for an integrated, balanced application of all instruments of U.S. national power.[219]

In late 2008, U.S. Embassy Kabul outlined a proposal for a "civilian surge" to support provincial- and local-level capacity-building in Afghanistan. The effort is intended to expand the U.S. government civilian field presence at U.S.-led PRTs and Task Forces. Experts are coming from the State Department, AID, USDA, and U.S. law enforcement agencies. The additional personnel are augmenting existing civilian staff functions and establishing a presence at the district level to help mentor sub-provincial-level GIRoA officials. During 2009, the number of U.S. civilian advisors in Afghanistan increased from about 300 to nearly 1,000, and Ambassador Holbrooke has estimated that an additional 300 will deploy during 2010. An FY2009 supplemental appropriation (P.L. 111-32) provided $600 million for this effort. In January 2010, Ambassador Holbrooke's office issued a report on the Afghanistan-Pakistan regional strategy that strongly emphasized the importance of this increased level of civilian assistance.[220]

---

[216] MG Jeffrey Schloesser, Interview, Bagram, Afghanistan, November 2008.

[217] MG Weigt, Interview, Mazar-e-Sharif, Afghanistan, November 2008.

[218] Sarah Chayes, "Clean up the Afghan Government, and the Taliban will Fade Away," *Washington Post*, December 14, 2008.

[219] See for example "Afghanistan: Winning the War. Problems, Solutions, and Critical Decisions for the Next Administration," Foundation for the Defense of Democracies, Washington DC, December 4, 2008, panel discussion video transcript available at http://www.defenddemocracy.org/index.php?option=com_content&view=article&id=11784099&Itemid=385.

[220] "Afghanistan-Pakistan Regional Stabilization Strategy," Office of the Special Representative for Afghanistan and Pakistan, p. 3. http://www.state.gov/documents/organization/135728.pdf

Future Options for the War in Afghanistan

Integrating the Overall Approach: Strategy and Implementation

Most Afghanistan observers have pointed to weaknesses in the coordination of the many disparate efforts to support Afghan security, governance or development, including ensuring that those three lines of operation complement one another. Some observers note that leaders of the primary international assistance efforts rarely speak with a unified voice, although their influence might be much stronger were they to do so. The scale of Afghanistan's needs, and the number and variety of entities offering help, make coordination a particularly great challenge.

To address the coordination challenge, some observers advocate crafting a new, overarching strategy for Afghanistan, which would state objectives for security, governance, and development; specify approaches; and assign roles and responsibilities for implementation. A new single set of guidelines, it is argued, would help focus cooperation and coordination.

Many practitioners and observers argue, however, that the basic contours of strategy are already in place. Importantly, GIRoA officials tend to agree with this view. The Afghanistan Compact, an agreement between the Government of Afghanistan (GIRoA) and the international community, identified basic objectives in each of the lines of operation. The 2008 Afghanistan National Development Strategy articulated a strategic vision and key objectives in security, governance, and development; provided multiple individual sector strategies under each of those headings; and stated guidelines for coordinating and monitoring implementation.[221] In the security arena, ISAF's 2008 Joint Campaign Plan (JCP) clearly stated objectives and approaches.

Experts have suggested two alternatives to writing a new strategy, in both of which the U.S. government could play a leadership role. One school of thought suggests that the specific language of a strategy document may be less important than the "buy-in" to its principles and approaches by all relevant players. In the case of Afghanistan, as former head of UNAMA Lakhdar Brahimi argued, those actors would include all of Afghanistan's neighbors, other regional leaders "including India, Iran, and Saudi Arabia," all permanent members of the UN Security Council, and all major donors including Japan.[222] What is needed, this school suggests, are intensified diplomatic efforts to forge a broad consensus on the basic contours of existing strategy.

Other experts have suggested a second option—accepting the basic tenets of existing strategy documents and focusing on strengthening monitoring and implementation. Diplomatic efforts might urge contributing countries to more rigorously tailor their assistance efforts to Afghan

---

[221] Afghanistan National Development Strategy 1387-1391 (2008-2013): A Strategy for Security, Governance, Economic Growth and Poverty Reduction, Islamic Republic of Afghanistan, 2008, available at http://www.ands.gov.af/ ands/ands_docs/index.asp.

[222] Lakhdar Brahimi, "A New Path for Afghanistan," Washington Post, December 7, 2008. The Afghanistan Study Group, which released its results in January 2008, called for developing not only "a long-term, coherent international strategy" but also "a strategic communications plan to garner strong public support for that strategy" among NATO countries and regional leaders. If "strategic communications" is regarded as two-way dialogue, then the Group's proposal is similar to Brahimi's. See General James L. Jones, USMC (ret), Ambassador Thomas R. Pickering, Co-Chairs, Afghanistan Study Group Report, "Revitalizing our Efforts, Rethinking our Strategies," Center for the Study of the Presidency, January 30, 2008, Page 11.

national priorities, or they might attempt to curb the "national-first" approach of those contributing countries that regularly lobby GIRoA ministers for attention to "their" provinces. New efforts might also support strengthening UNAMA so that it might more effectively play its critical coordination role as co-chair of the Joint Coordination and Monitoring Board (JCMB), tasked to oversee coordinate implementation of the Afghanistan Compact.

Adjusting U.S. and Other International Forces

In 2008 and 2009, NATO and U.S. commanders on the ground in Afghanistan requested additional international forces—requests echoed by GIRoA officials. Key policy questions include the scope of the requirement, the likely duration of the requirement, and the options, including possible combinations of U.S. and other NATO forces, for meeting the requirement.

For those who advocate troop level increases, the duration of the need for higher international troop levels in Afghanistan is hard to determine in advance. Future requirements might depend on changes in the strength of the insurgency, growth in the capacity and capabilities of the ANSF, adaptations in the approaches used by international forces, and concurrent progress in the areas of governance and development. General McKiernan has argued that international troop levels need to be increased until the "tipping point" is reached when the ANSF assume lead security responsibility—"three or four more years away."[223] To be clear, Afghan and U.S. officials do not use the term "surge," arguing that "surge" refers to a temporary increase in troop strength, while the requirement in Afghanistan is likely to last for some time.[224]

Requirement for Additional Forces?

A first premise of counterinsurgency is conducting operations "by, with and through" indigenous forces. Where such forces are not available, international forces may substitute, support, and/or help build additional indigenous forces. The military effort in Afghanistan was, from the start, an "economy of force" mission, in terms of both international troop strength, and early target endstrength goals for the Afghan National Security Forces (ANSF). That approach provided only limited geographical coverage of Afghanistan. Commanders on the ground, such as General McChrystal, have maintained that significant additional forces are needed to meet the full scope of requirements.

At the same time, some key observers have argued against additional U.S. or other international force deployments, on the grounds of general Afghan antipathy to the presence of foreign forces on their soil, exacerbated by any episodes of heavy-handedness by those forces. Thus, they suggest additional deployments will actually prove counterproductive to the COIN effort. Regional expert Rory Stewart has argued flatly, "the West should not increase troop numbers," because doing so would inflame Afghan nationalism and lend support to the insurgency. "The Taliban," he adds, "which was a largely discredited and backward movement, gains support by portraying itself as fighting for Islam and Afghanistan against a foreign military occupation."[225]

---

[223] Tom Vanden Brook, "A 'Tough Fight' Seem for Afghan War in '09," *USA Today,* December 8, 2009.

[224] Tom Vanden Brook, "A 'Tough Fight' Seem for Afghan War in '09," *USA Today*, December 8, 2009. Vanden Brook interviews General McKiernan, whom he quotes as saying: "I don't like to use the word surge here because if we put these additional forces in here, it's going to be for the next few years. It's not a temporary increase of combat strength."

[225] See Rory Stewart, "How to Save Afghanistan," *Time*, July 17, 2008. Stewart, the author of *The Places in Between,* (continued...)

Noted regional scholar Barnett Rubin has argued, similarly, that the "Afghans don't like their country being occupied by foreign soldiers any more than did their ancestors," and that reaching a political solution to the insurgency "may require decreasing the U.S. and other foreign military presence rather than increasing it."[226]

NATO Forces

One option for meeting any identified requirements for additional forces is through contributions from NATO Allies. Key considerations include both the likelihood and the utility of additional NATO contributions.

Some experts have raised questions about the utility of possible contributions from some NATO Allies, given the national caveats that still tightly constrain the activities of many contingents. One option for the U.S. government would be to continue to press Allies to relax or eliminate such caveats—Secretary of State Clinton has indicated that the Obama Administration intends to pursue this approach.[227] One alternative in some cases would be to focus on contributions less likely to create domestic political opposition. Some contributors, for example, might provide so-called "niche" capabilities such as explosive ordnance disposal (EOD) expertise and medical facilities, while others might choose to "sponsor"—that is, pay for and run—branch schools used for training the Afghan National Army.

U.S. Forces

The most likely avenue, however, for meeting any requirements for additional international forces is an increase in U.S. troop strength in Afghanistan. As of the beginning of 2009, an additional brigade combat team (BCT)—3rd BCT, 10th Mountain Division—was flowing into Regional Command-East, and General McKiernan had requested three additional BCTs or equivalents, plus an aviation brigade and all the necessary enablers., General McChrystal increased this request to up to nine additional BCTs, or roughly 40,000 troops. After the latest strategy review, President Obama has authorized the deployment of an additional six BCTs (30,000+) troops.

Observers have raised several different concerns about the ramifications of substantially increasing the U.S. share of the total ISAF force, as well as strengthening the U.S. role in ISAF command and control arrangements. The more prominent the U.S. role, some argue, the less likely that Allies will increase or perhaps even sustain their own contributions, since it will be easier for them to argue that the United States is meeting the requirement. Other skeptics point to a potential operational challenge—the possibility of a *de facto* bifurcation of Afghanistan into two distinct sets of approaches, robust COIN by the United States and a few Allies in eastern and southern Afghanistan, and softer stability operations by all other Allies and partners in northern and western Afghanistan. Such visible disparity, if it emerged, would make it much harder for ISAF to speak with a unified voice to GIRoA. Many civilian and military senior ISAF officials

---

(...continued)

is a former British diplomat and the head of the Turquoise Mountain project in Kabul.

[226] Barnett R. Rubin, "Afghan Dilemmas: Defining Commitments," *The American Interest,* vol. 3, no.5 (May/June 2008), pp.45-46.

[227] See the replies to questions for the record, submitted by Secretary of State nominee Hillary Clinton to the Senate Foreign Relations Committee (SFRC), for her January 13, 2009, confirmation hearing, available at http://www.foreignpolicy.com/files/KerryClintonQFRs.pdf.

---

from non-U.S. Allies gently caution that, at the very least, the United States should avoid suggesting that the increased U.S. role was made necessary by inadequacies in the performance of their Allies.

Logistics

The deployment of additional U.S. forces is likely to raise significant logistics challenges. U.S. forces based in eastern and southern Afghanistan have relied heavily to date on lines of communication (LOC) running across Afghanistan's mountainous eastern border into Pakistan, and down to the port city of Karachi. According to ISAF officials, with increased force flow, the demand on those LOCs is likely to increase by 500%, posing challenges in terms of both capacity and security. In late 2008, a series of insurgent attacks on those LOCs, on the Pakistani side of the border, underscored their vulnerability. In addition, the Government of Pakistan (GoP) has occasionally closed the primary border crossing, at the Khyber Pass, ostensibly to support GoP military operations in border regions. "Our biggest vulnerability," said one ISAF senior official, "is our LOCs."[228]

One alternative is the use of northern supply routes through former Soviet republics north of Afghanistan. On January 20, 2009, General Petraeus, CENTCOM Commanding General, announced that new agreements had been reached with Russia and Central Asian states regarding the transit of goods and supplies to Afghanistan. These arrangements are intended to complement the Pakistani supply routes—General Petraeus commented, "It is very important as we increase the effort in Afghanistan that we have multiple routes that go into the country."[229] Some experts have raised a concern about this option—the uncertainty about Russia's future orientation, its support for the international effort in Afghanistan, and the influence it might choose to exercise over any Central Asian support to that effort.

One additional practical consideration is the additional requirement for contractors resulting from increased U.S. troop deployments. ISAF officials noted in late 2008 that the U.S. Army had insufficient engineering assets available to support the construction in southern Afghanistan required by the arrival of large numbers of additional U.S. troops. They added that the availability of local contractors in southern Afghanistan was already scarce, given that the limited pool of qualified personnel was already occupied with work for ISAF and other organizations.

Sourcing U.S. Deployments

With concurrent wars in Afghanistan and Iraq, the Department of Defense (DOD) could find it a challenge to source and then sustain larger troop deployments to Afghanistan.

One ramification could be delays in the arrival of additional forces in theater. DOD leaders indicated in late 2008 that DOD was working to send additional military forces to Afghanistan but that it would take some time—perhaps half a year—for them to become available. Senior U.S.

---

[228] ISAF official, Interview, Kabul, Afghanistan, November 2008. Recent attacks on the supply line from Karachi, Pakistan, to the Afghanistan border included the December 7, 2008, insurgent attacks on two truck stops in Peshawar, Pakistan, destroying over 100 vehicles with supplies bound for Afghanistan, and the November 10, 2008, insurgent hijacking of a convoy of vehicles on the road to the Khyber pass, bound for Afghanistan. See Laura King, "Suspected Taliban Militants Destroy Supply Trucks," *Los Angeles Times*, December 8, 2008.

[229] Chris Brummitt, "U.S. Reaches Deal on Afghan Supply Routes," *Army Times*, January 20, 2009.

---

military officials have indicated that additional force flow into Afghanistan is connected to U.S. force drawdowns in Iraq. Some observers note that such a delay may not prove neutral—that even if the insurgency is held to what some practitioners call its current "stalemate," Afghan popular opinion, the center of gravity in COIN, may well slide toward greater disaffection.

A second implication could be a continuation of stress on parts of the force. Numerous defense strategists have commented on the stress that simultaneous wars in Afghanistan and Iraq have placed on U.S. military forces, and particularly on the Army and Marine Corps. That pressure has manifested itself in repeated and extended deployments for both units and individual servicemembers, and has affected the personal lives of individual servicemembers through medical conditions and stress on families.

One key decision concerning additional U.S. force flow to Afghanistan will be the mix of Military Services and in particular, the Army and Marine Corps. The Marine Corps has long advocated a transition of its primary focus from Iraq to Afghanistan, arguing that improved security conditions in Anbar province, its area of responsibility in Iraq, allow a drawdown, and that Marine warfighting capabilities are especially well-suited for the growing security challenges in southern Afghanistan.[230]

A further decision concerns the type of Army combat forces that would deploy. To date, the U.S. Army has deployed "light" combat units to Afghanistan. If the Army continues to provide the majority of U.S. forces in Afghanistan, and if the decision is to continue to deploy exclusively light combat units, then stress on the infantry could become acute. One option might be the introduction of heavy BCTs, but their capabilities might be less well-suited for Afghanistan's terrain.

Updating Counterinsurgency (COIN) Approaches

Counterinsurgency approaches, by definition, require continual adaptation to the local environment.

One set of COIN military strategy questions in Afghanistan concerns population security, and in particular, how best to balance the need to maintain a dispersed footprint, living among the population, given the antipathy of some parts of that population toward any foreign presence. In Afghanistan, this dilemma has been particularly evident in some isolated mountain valleys. One option is to sustain an international troop presence, coupled with development and governance assistance, aiming to win over the local population eventually. An alternative—diametrically opposed both theoretically and practically—is to accept that "population security" may not work identically in every context, to withdraw the antagonizing foreign force presence in some

---

[230] See Otto Kreisher, "Marine Commandant Expects Troop Surge in Afghanistan," *National Journal*, January 15, 2009. See also Gordon Lubold, "A 'Surge' for Afghanistan?, The Christian Science Monitor, November 29, 2007; Lubold cited General James Conway, Commandant of the Marine Corps, as saying: "The trend lines tell us that it may be time to increase the force posture in Afghanistan. …If it requires additional US forces, then it goes back to our suggestion that maybe we need more Marines in there with a more kinetic bent." General Conway has also expressed concern that the Marines have "become, in some ways, a second land army," and may be losing their "expeditionary flavor," a danger that deployment to Afghanistan might help to avert. See Remarks by General James T. Conway, Commandant of the Marine Corps, Center for a New American Security, Washington DC, October 15, 2007, Available at http://www.marines.mil/units/hqmc/cmc/Documents/Speeches20071015CNAS.pdf.

locations, and to sacrifice some measure of security against insurgents for a different kind of stability—an absence of discord between foreign forces and the local population.

Another set of options concerns possible adjustments to the use of kinetic air operations in Afghanistan. The year 2008 witnessed sharp criticism from GIRoA and UNAMA of civilian casualties caused by air strikes. Such incidents have the potential to sharply discourage popular support for the government, essential to the success of any counterinsurgency. In late 2008, ISAF updated its Tactical Directive, carefully articulating rules for the use of fires. In 2009, General McChrystal reiterated the importance of reducing or eliminating civilian casualties in his August ISAF Commander's Counterinsurgency Guidance.[231] The year 2010 may prove a good test of the impact on civilian casualties of the new guidelines, and of a larger international forces presence that may allow some reduction in the use of kinetic air power.

A further set of options concerns the balance of effort between Special Operations Forces (SOF) and conventional forces. Some experts have argued that the military effort in Afghanistan would benefit from boosting the role of SOF vis-à-vis conventional forces. In Afghanistan, SOF play the lead role in targeting insurgent leaders, and proponents argue that increasing SOF troop strength might lead to more targeting successes. Other experts counter that successful SOF efforts rely on international conventional forces and the ANSF, both to provide information about a battlespace in advance, and to "hold" that battlespace after kinetic operations. That collaborative partnership, they argue, is essential to the success of overall COIN efforts, and therefore, the utility of unilateral increases in SOF deployments for the overall COIN mission would be limited.

Developing the Afghan National Security Forces (ANSF)

Experts generally agree that the development of the Afghan National Security Forces is essential to the future security and stability of Afghanistan.[232] In late 2008, GIRoA, backed by the support of the international community, decided to increase the target endstrength of the Afghan National Army (ANA). Further major policy issues include the size of the total ANSF, the mix of forces within it, the focus of effort of those forces, the timeline for developing those forces, and funding further ANSF development.

Practitioners underscore that ANSF development is highly dynamic. As Afghan National Police (ANP) capabilities grow, the ANP may increasingly assume responsibility for some domestic missions now performed by the Afghan National Army (ANA). As total ANSF numbers and capabilities grow, Afghan forces may increasingly assume responsibility from international security forces. And when—as expected—the security challenges from the insurgency diminish, the ANSF may shift from COIN to more traditional peacetime foci, including external defense for the ANA, and civilian law enforcement for the ANP.

---

[231] ISAF Commander's Counterinsurgency Guidance, August 2009, ISAF Headquarters, may be found at http://www.nato.int/isaf/docu/official_texts/counterinsurgency_guidance.pdf.

[232] See General James L. Jones, USMC (ret), Ambassador Thomas R. Pickering, *Afghanistan Study Group Report: Revitalizing our Efforts, Rethinking our Strategies,* Center for the Study of the Presidency, January 30, 2008, p.23. The authors argued for an enhanced international effort: "The U.S. and its NATO partners also need to focus more efforts and resources on training and standing up the Afghan National Army and recruiting, training, and providing adequate pay and equipment to the Afghan National Police so they can maintain security in an area once coalition forces depart."

One critical issue is funding the development and sustainment of the ANSF. Senior Afghan and international officials estimate that it will cost approximately $3.5 billion per year to increase ANSF force structure, and then $2.2 billion per year to sustain it. Unlike Iraq, whose oil revenues have funded an increasing share of the costs of growing and sustaining the Iraqi Security Forces in recent years, Afghanistan has few natural resources and little economic activity, other than poppy production, that could generate significant revenue in the near future. GIRoA, which contributed $320 million to the ANSF in 2008, is not a realistic source of ANSF funding in the near term.[233] International support, and particularly U.S. support, is expected to bear the near-term burden of developing the ANSF, until it reaches its current endstrength targets.

Growing the ANA to 134,000—or more—raises the twin questions of funding and sustainability. It is expected that the currently planned ANA growth will be funded by the international community; the United States is currently the leading contributor. If GIRoA wanted to sustain the force beyond that time frame, theoretical options would include continued U.S. and international support, or Afghan assumption of some level of financial responsibility. Alternatives could include demobilizing some part of the force—if GIRoA had the ability to do so—or, hypothetically, making part of the force available to serve in multi-lateral peace operations, in which case the international community might bear some of its costs.

For the future, one option, in the absence of GIRoA ability to shoulder the burden, would be sustained international support, a responsibility likely to fall to the U.S. government, based on current patterns. The policy question for the U.S. government, in turn, would concern whether national interests support sustaining that sizable commitment—and if so, at what levels, and for how long.

In the absence of either Afghan or international funding sources, one option would be demobilizing some part of the Afghan forces. A conclusive defeat of insurgent forces might increase the plausibility of such an approach, by reducing the requirement for ANSF numbers for the COIN fight. One challenge could prove to be limited ability on the part of the Afghan civilian leadership to direct the security ministries to decrease their forces.

One additional option, with some cost implications, would be a future role for Afghanistan as net exporter of security, providing trained, interoperable ANSF to serve in UN peace operations or other multi-national coalition efforts around the world. Minister of Defense Wardak suggested this possibility by noting, "One day we will pay our debt by fighting shoulder to shoulder with you," words that might apply abroad as well as at home.[234] Playing such roles might help GIRoA secure some international support for maintaining its force.

A further policy issue concerning the ANSF is force modernization—including the likely future requirements the ANSF will face, and the steps the ANSF might begin taking now, in terms of training and procurement, to prepare to meet those future requirements. While army and police commanders on the ground are fully focused on the current fight, Minister of Defense Wardak has argued in favor of beginning to build a mix of forces that would also be appropriate to the post-COIN environment. One implication for the U.S. government is the impact GIRoA force modernization decisions may have on foreign military sales requests.

---

[233] MG Robert Cone, Interview, Kabul, Afghanistan, November 2008.

[234] Minister of Defense of Afghanistan Abdul Rahim Wardak, Interview, Kabul, Afghanistan, November 2008.

One final consideration concerning the development of the ANSF, is the nature of emerging civil-military relationships within the Government of Afghanistan. Some civil-military experts caution that there is an inherent danger, when a state's army is by far its most competent, effective organization, that civilian control of the military may erode. In late 2008, some Afghan officials, including Minister of Defense Wardak, have pointed to a tendency on the part of President Karzai to ask the ANA to play non-military roles—for example, guarding civilian prisons—when civilian personnel are unavailable. U.S. military officials have noted that they spend significant time with senior Afghan security officials, mentoring them on the role of security forces in a democracy.[235]

Addressing Regional Issues

By the end of 2008, a near-consensus had emerged among practitioners and observers that the challenges Afghanistan faces could not be successfully addressed without a "regional" approach. Policy options might include various avenues for influencing the behavior of neighboring states, particularly Pakistan and Iran, in order to shape the security climate in Afghanistan. Some but not all commentators argue, in addition, that because Pakistan and India tend to make use of Afghanistan as a pawn in their own long-simmering conflict, successful "regional" initiatives concerning Afghanistan must also take into account the Pakistan-India relationship. Some commentators also suggest that Iraq is germane as a major security preoccupation for Iran, whose behavior in Afghanistan may be affected by developments across its opposite border. While the exhortation to consider the broader region has widespread support, no consensus on regional strategy has emerged—to date, experts have put forward a very wide range of specific policy prescriptions, some of them mutually contradictory.

Pakistan

The U.S. government may wish to address both strategic and operational policy options concerning Pakistan's role vis-à-vis Afghanistan.

At the strategic level, a central question concerns the most effective ways to encourage Pakistani action against those supporting and fomenting the Afghanistan insurgency. One group of experts urges assistance efforts to support governance and development in "the impoverished areas that have become breeding grounds for militants," in particular along the border, in order to diminish the generation of, and support for, insurgents.[236] This could be of particular importance if intensified counterinsurgency operations in Afghanistan drive insurgents across the border into Pakistan. Enhance coordination with the Pakistani military could go some distance toward mitigating this concern, though any such coordination may be constrained by operational security requirements.

Several other groups of experts particularly emphasize the importance of the U.S.-Pakistani mil-to-mil relationship, as a tool for shaping Pakistani actions. Some argue that the key is to continue to build Pakistani capabilities and to shape their orientation by strengthening current initiatives—for example, by boosting U.S. efforts to train the Pakistan Army Special Forces for counter-terrorism operations, expanding Pakistani participation in military exchange programs, and

---

[235] MG Robert Cone, Interview, Kabul, Afghanistan, November 2008.

[236] Christopher D. Kolenda, "How to Win in Afghanistan," *Weekly Standard*, October 13, 2008. Colonel Christopher Kolenda recently commanded a U.S. Army battalion in Afghanistan along the border with Pakistan.

fostering closer mil-to-mil coordination along the Afghanistan-Pakistan border.[237] Others agree that mil-to-mil initiatives are key but urge making the provision of the benefits they offer conditional on stronger Pakistani support along the border with Afghanistan.[238] Some experts, in contrast, argue that the close U.S.-Pakistan mil-to-mil relationship is part of the problem, as it may tend to diminish Pakistani civilian control over its military. Therefore, one regional expert writes, "the United States must relinquish, not strengthen, the privileged relationship between the United States and the Pakistani military."[239]

Another set of experts argues that efforts to shape Pakistani actions vis-à-vis Afghanistan are likely to be successful only as part of a broader approach to Pakistan's concerns and its role in the region. Key issues, in this broader perspective, might include Pakistan's role as a nuclear power, and its tendentious relationship with nuclear-armed neighbor India—in particular their rival claims to the disputed territory of Kashmir. Policy options might include, for example, more robust U.S. unilateral, or multilateral, diplomatic efforts to help India and Pakistan forge a stable, sustainable relationship.

The Obama Administration has indicated initial support for a Pakistan policy that includes both increasing non-military aid, and conditioning the provision of mil-to-mil assistance on Pakistani actions such as "...clos[ing] down training camps, evict[ing] foreign fighters, and prevent[ing] the Taliban and al Qaeda from using Pakistan as a sanctuary."[240]

Meanwhile, at the operational level, a key question is whether to continue U.S. cross-border attacks while strategic-level dialogue and other attempts to exercise leverage are underway. Continued cross-border attacks might lead to political blow-back in Pakistan, but they might also persuade Pakistani officials to take more decisive steps to end support to insurgents. Options, therefore, might include either accelerating or decreasing the use of cross-border attacks. Options might also include seeking additional avenues for strengthening tactical-level cross-border coordination, including increasing the frequency or scope of regular coordination meetings, establishing further border coordination centers, and improving the ease of tactical-level coordination in actions against insurgent targets.

---

[237] See Thomas Lynch, "Afghan Dilemmas: Staying Power," *The American Interest,* vol. 3, no.5 (May/June 2008), p.36. U.S. Army Colonel Thomas Lynch has served in Afghanistan.

[238] See Vikram J. Singh and Nathaniel C. Fick, "Surging Statecraft to Save Afghanistan," *Small Wars Journal,* October 2, 2008.

[239] Barnett R. Rubin, "Afghan Dilemmas: Defining Commitments," *The American Interest,* vol. 3, no.5 (May/June 2008), p.49. He adds that the United States "must instead support civilian control over the government and military alike, even by parties that oppose U.S. objectives openly (rather than covertly, like the military)."

[240] See the replies to questions for the record, submitted by Secretary of State nominee Hillary Clinton to the Senate Foreign Relations Committee (SFRC), for her January 13, 2009, confirmation hearing, available at http://www.foreignpolicy.com/files/KerryClintonQFRs.pdf. Under Secretary of Defense for Policy Michèle Flournoy, in replies to questions for the record submitted for her own confirmation hearing, with the Senate Armed Services Committee on January 15, 2009, echoed the same premise, stating: "The U.S. must have an integrated strategy to promote development and prevent terrorism across the Afghanistan-Pakistan border region." See replies to questions for the record, submitted by Under Secretary of Defense for Policy nominee to the Senate Armed Services Committee (SASC), for her January 15, 2009, confirmation hearing, available at http://armed-services.senate.gov/statemnt/2009/January/Flournoy%2001-15-09.pdf.

Iran

Practitioners and observers recognize Iran's dual track role in Afghanistan—providing both humanitarian and lethal aid. The key issue in U.S. Afghanistan policy debates is how best to leverage concerns that Iran shares with the rest of the international community—including regional security and the impact of the narcotics trade—to shape Iranian choices.

Options include a more concerted diplomatic outreach to Tehran, by the United States and/or other members of the international community, designed to build on shared regional concerns. Some experts suggest that Tehran may be more likely to respond positively to outreach efforts by the Obama Administration, than to those by its predecessor. Another option—not mutually exclusive—is robust countering of any Iranian efforts to provide lethal aid to insurgents in Afghanistan.

Strengthening Counternarcotics Efforts

Despite the existence of broadly agreed counternarcotics (CN) strategies, and some recent declines in cultivation, many practitioners see little likelihood of significant further CN progress until GIRoA takes major further strides in establishing the rule of law, including both building a formal judicial system and encouraging a pervasive law-based culture. Some observers have further suggested that there may be inherent contradictions between CN and COIN efforts, since a key premise of COIN is fostering popular support for the government, while some CN initiatives may alienate parts of the population, at least temporarily.

One near term option is for GIRoA and ISAF to take full advantage of the October 2008 NATO decision expanding the interpretation of the CN role ISAF may play, to include targeting drug facilities when a connection with the insurgency can be shown. Focused diplomatic efforts might prove useful in persuading some Allies to fully embrace this broader interpretation.

A further option might be more assiduously cultivating the cooperation of community as well as provincial leaders in CN efforts, including strengthening the system of incentives available to those who lend their support. The Afghanistan Social Outreach Program, designed to foster and focus ground-up capacity-building, might naturally complement any such outreach efforts.

Achieving a NATO Success in Afghanistan?

Most NATO observers suggest that "Afghanistan" is a critical test for the Alliance, including its ability to conduct major out-of-area missions, and its relevance to 21st century security challenges, and many have argued that failure in Afghanistan could spell the end of the Alliance. In January 2008, the Afghanistan Study Group argued, "A failure of the NATO mission in Afghanistan would also damage the future prospects of the organization itself."[241] For a number of practitioners, that line of thinking implies an imperative to make sure that the Alliance is successful in Afghanistan—which is not quite the same thing, logically, as making sure that Afghanistan itself succeeds. Key policy considerations include what it would take for the

---

[241] See for example General James L. Jones, USMC (ret), Ambassador Thomas R. Pickering, *Afghanistan Study Group Report: Revitalizing our Efforts, Rethinking our Strategies,* Center for the Study of the Presidency, January 30, 2008, Page 17.

outcome in Afghanistan to be considered a "NATO success," and what if any differences that might entail from a strict pursuit of security, good governance and development for Afghanistan. In some circumstances, U.S. policy-makers might choose to weigh the imperative of accomplishing the mission against the imperative to support NATO as an institution.

Some observers suggest that the growing presence of U.S. forces, and possibly a stronger U.S. role in ISAF command and control, may lead to the perception that any progress in Afghanistan is due to U.S. rather than NATO efforts. In that vein, the Afghanistan Study Group argued, "Burden-sharing among NATO allies is critical to the mission in terms of both available resources and public perceptions—an increasingly unilateral mission will be politically vulnerable in Afghanistan, the U.S., and NATO."[242] Options for countering such perceptions, if so desired, might include maintaining U.S. battlespace-owning units under ISAF command; using diplomatic channels to forge stronger consensus on the nature and stakes of the fight in Afghanistan; and soliciting non-military forms of assistance from those countries unwilling or unable to provide large ground force contingents for the counterinsurgency fight.

Supporting Reconciliation

A number of key practitioners and observers have supported "reconciliation" outreach initiatives, to insurgent leaders and/or their foot soldiers, as one avenue toward final settlement of the conflict in Afghanistan. Senior U.S. military officials in Afghanistan underscore that questions concerning to whom to reach out, at what time, with what offers, and with what endstate in view, are policy matters for GIRoA decision. Any "reconciliation" efforts would likely have a direct bearing on security efforts in Afghanistan, because they concern the formal adversary—the insurgents—in the fight.

Some experts have argued that leadership-level reconciliation initiatives risk institutionalizing formal political roles in the future Government of Afghanistan for known "bad guys." Such inclusion, they suggest, might alienate parts of the Afghan population who suffered repression under the Taliban regime. Worse, such alienated constituencies might take up arms to protest such brokered deals. Institutionalizing leading roles for former Taliban or other insurgent leaders might also, it is suggested, push the orientation of the Government of Afghanistan in more repressive directions.

U.S. government policy considerations might include determining the U.S. preferred outcome of any such talks, and exercising diplomacy to influence the form and content of any such initiatives. From an operational perspective, U.S. deliberations might include assessing how different military strategies might contribute to bringing Taliban leaders to the negotiations table in a frame of mind conducive to agreeing to conditions acceptable to GIRoA. For example, Taliban leaders might be compelled to come to terms by even more aggressive targeting, or by more strident efforts to cut off the funding support they receive from the narcotics trade.

---

[242] General James L. Jones, USMC (ret), Ambassador Thomas R. Pickering, *Afghanistan Study Group Report: Revitalizing our Efforts, Rethinking our Strategies,* Center for the Study of the Presidency, January 30, 2008, Page 17.

Applying the Lessons of Afghanistan to Future Force Development

For the longer term, defense practitioners and analysts are likely to continue to seek lessons from U.S. military prosecution of the wars in Afghanistan and Iraq to apply to future U.S. force shaping and sizing. Such conclusions, and they way they are applied, are likely to have a profound impact on how the Military Services fulfill their responsibilities, in accordance with Title 10, U.S. Code, to organize, man, train and equip military forces. Critical policy considerations for DOD are likely to include the capabilities required to successfully prosecute complex contingency operations like those in Afghanistan and Iraq, the likelihood that the United States will engage in similar complex contingencies in the future, and the relative importance of such skills compared to more traditional military capabilities.

The publication of Department of Defense Directive 3000.07 on "Irregular Warfare," in December 2008, which stated that "IW is as strategically important as traditional warfare," reflected and helped institutionalize a growing DOD emphasis on complex contingency capabilities.[243]

Should this school of thought continue to hold sway, options might include further increasing the endstrength of the ground forces, and raising the profile of the mission to train and advise foreign security forces. In a resource-constrained environment, any such choices would like entail trade-offs with other DOD capability areas.

Balancing and Integrating Civilian and Military Efforts

Years of operational experience in Afghanistan, like those in Iraq, have helped fuel debates about appropriately balancing military and civilian capabilities in the U.S. government, and effectively integrating those capabilities with each other.

A key short-term policy consideration is the U.S. government response to the appeal from U.S. Embassy Kabul for further civilian resources—personnel and ready funds—to support capacity-building efforts in Afghanistan. One constraint may be the availability of trained civilian personnel with the appropriate expertise, ready to deploy. Another constraint may be the availability of funds—in particular, civilian funding streams relatively free of bureaucratic red tape that allow quick execution.

Some U.S. commanders on the ground, while generally welcoming the prospect of civilian expertise, caution that such an initiative would be most valuable if it carefully recruits people with relevant expertise. Simply "throwing bodies at the problem," they caution, would not be helpful. Some add that it would also be important to ensure that additional civilian personnel are included in clear civilian chains of command, to ensure unity of effort among their various activities.

---

[243] Department of Defense, "Irregular Warfare (IW)," DoDD 3000.07, December 1, 2008. The Directive defined IW this way: "A violent struggle among state and non-state actors for legitimacy and influence over the relevant population(s). Irregular warfare favors indirect and asymmetric approaches, though it may employ the full range of military and other capacities, in order to erode an adversary's power, influence, and will." It noted that "IW can include a variety of steady-state and surge DoD activities and operations: counter-terrorism, unconventional warfare; foreign internal defense; counterinsurgency; and stability operations that, in the context of IW, involve establishing or re-establishing order in a fragile state."

Some outside experts, in turn, caution against any infusion of civilian personnel that might detract from GIRoA efforts to govern their own country. One regional expert, arguing that the U.S. government should not increase its involvement in the Afghan government or economy, has written: "The more responsibility we take in Afghanistan, the more we undermine the credibility and responsibility of the Afghan government and encourage it to act irresponsibly."[244] Another expert has urged, "Rather than sending in thousands of civilians, the shift in emphasis could be to training Afghans to do the jobs themselves."[245] U.S. Embassy appeals for a "civilian surge" are predicated on precisely that advisory approach.

Key policy considerations for the longer-term, suggested by U.S. experience in Afghanistan, might include whether the U.S. government requires increased civilian capacity to meet possible future complex contingency requirements, and if so, what capabilities would be required, and how might they best be cultivated and organized. A related consideration concerns the implications of any enhancement of U.S. government civilian capacity for military requirements—whether, for example, increased civilian capacity might decrease the missions military forces should be prepared to accomplish. And finally, regardless of the balance in numbers and capabilities between military and civilian personnel, a further policy consideration is how best to effectively integrate military and civilian complex contingency efforts, in both planning and execution.

Additional Reports

CRS Report RL33110, *The Cost of Iraq, Afghanistan, and Other Global War on Terror Operations Since 9/11*, by Amy Belasco.

CRS Report RL32686, *Afghanistan: Narcotics and U.S. Policy*, by Christopher M. Blanchard.

CRS Report RL33627, *NATO in Afghanistan: A Test of the Transatlantic Alliance*, by Vincent Morelli and Paul Belkin.

CRS Report RL30588, *Afghanistan: Post-Taliban Governance, Security, and U.S. Policy*, by Kenneth Katzman.

CRS Report RL33498, *Pakistan-U.S. Relations*, by K. Alan Kronstadt.

---

[244] Rory Stewart, "How to Save Afghanistan," *Time,* July 17, 2008.

[245] Clare Lockhart, "Learning from Experience," *Slate,* November 5, 2008.

Figure 1. Map of Afghanistan

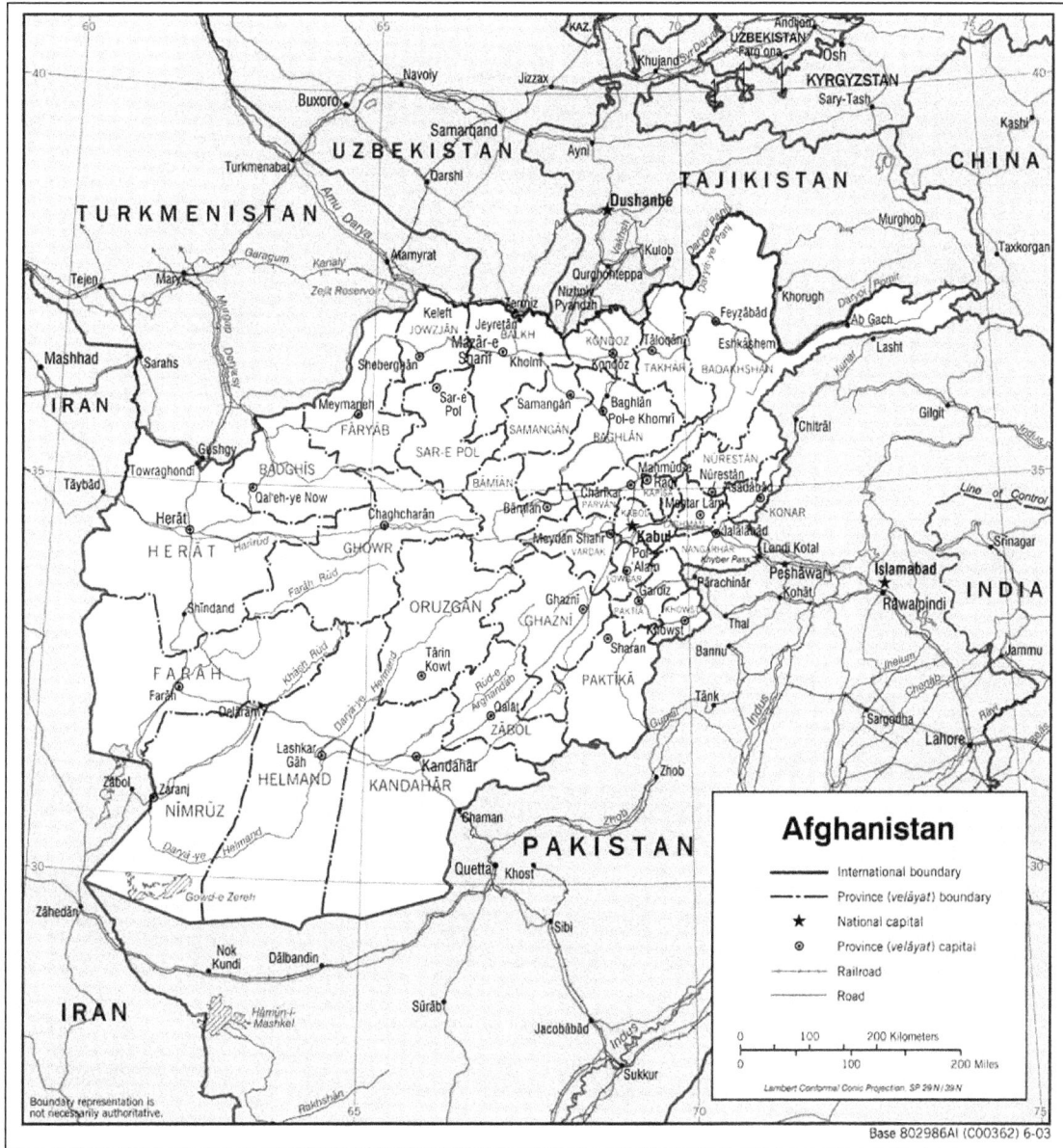

Source: The University of Texas at Austin, Perry-Castañeda Library Map Collection, Afghanistan Political Map 2003.

Author Contact Information

Steve Bowman
Specialist in National Security
sbowman@crs.loc.gov, 7-5841

Catherine Dale
Specialist in International Security

www.ingramcontent.com/pod-product-compliance
Lightning Source LLC
Chambersburg PA
CBHW050906100426
42737CB00048B/3231